What Drives Quality

A Deep Dive into Software Quality with Practical Solutions for Delivering High-Quality Products

Ben Linders

This book is for sale at http://leanpub.com/WhatDrivesQuality

This version was published on 2017-12-30

ISBN 978-94-92119-17-9

Leanpub

This is a Leanpub book. Leanpub empowers authors and publishers with the Lean Publishing process. Lean Publishing is the act of publishing an in-progress ebook using lightweight tools and many iterations to get reader feedback, pivot until you have the right book and build traction once you do.

Tweet This Book!

Please help Ben Linders by spreading the word about this book on Twitter!

The suggested tweet for this book is:

I'm reading "What Drives Quality". Get your own copy! benlinders.com/what-drives-quality #DriveQuality

The suggested hashtag for this book is #DriveQuality.

Find out what other people are saying about the book by clicking on this link to search for this hashtag on Twitter:

#DriveQuality

Contents

CONTENTS

Foreword

Ben Linders states in his Preface that quality is not a "sexy" topic. In fact, IT executives yawn when you mention "quality", and start checking email on their smartphones. Even so, another term for quality is "risk". Having entered the era of 9-digit defects (not bits or bytes, rather Euros or dollars), the risk exposure of poor quality software has implications for the quarterly financials. The CEO, not the CIO, is now answering for the effects of poor quality software.

Most of the recent €100 million IT outages and security breaches are traced back to defects in the software. Some defects, such as the all too frequent SQL Injection vulnerabilities, have been well-known since the last century. So why do developers still make these mistakes? And why are they not caught before being placed into production?

Too often the answer is an "I need it yesterday" mentality, exacerbated by a lack of professional discipline. This book delves into the factors that affect quality at every step of the software development cycle. It then describes practices that help development teams gain control of them to produce dependable, trustworthy software. Consequently, these practices reduce the risk to operations and the cost of maintenance.

Since most IT organizations report they are implementing some form of iterative/agile/DevOps development process, this book focuses on adopting quality practices in agile environments. In fact, half of the book is devoted to agile quality techniques. Ben's objective is to make sure the speed of delivery is matched by the speed of assurance.

This book is not a compendium of everything known about software quality. Rather it is a succinct summary of what we know and

i

how to apply it. It can be read in "agile time", and delivers a solid overview that can set readers on course to higher quality, lower risk software. Start here, then follow Ben's recommended readings if you want a deeper dive into specific quality topics. This book is a valuable contribution to professional software engineering practice.

Dr. Bill Curtis
Executive Director, Consortium for IT Software Quality
Fort Worth, Texas

Preface

I'm an active blogger at www.benlinders.com. On my blog, I share my experiences on agile and lean topics, including software quality.

I published my first book on Valuable Agile Retrospectives in 2013. This book – Getting Value out of Agile Retrospectives – has become a huge success. It has many readers all over the world and has been translated by agile teams of volunteers into 13 languages already.

Many readers have told me that they value my blog posts on quality. In 2014 I started writing my second book and decided that the topic should be software quality.

The book started from the blog post series What Drives Quality which is based on the research that I did with the Software Engineering Institute (SEI) and my experience working as quality and process manager in large organizations.

The first editions of this book were a kind of Minimum Viable Product to find out if people are actually interested in software quality. From the feedback that I received, I found out that there is an audience for this book – there are sufficient readers who feel that quality matters.

However, I also found out that quality is not a "sexy" topic. Since it's hard to develop high-quality products many people avoid the topic. Opinions vary on what quality is and isn't and what can be done to ingrain quality into the way products are developed.

A book on quality should be practical. It should help you, reader of this book, to improve the quality of your software and deliver better products. It should inspire you and give you energy to persevere on your quality journey. What Drives Quality tries to do just that, and more.

This book is based on my experience as a developer, tester, team leader, project manager, quality manager, process manager, consultant, coach, trainer, and adviser in Agile, Lean, Quality and Continuous Improvement. It takes a deep dive into quality with views from different perspectives and provides ideas, suggestions, practices, and experiences that will help you to improve quality of the products that your organization is delivering.

I'm aiming this book at software developers and testers, architects, product owners and managers, agile coaches, Scrum masters, project managers, and operational and senior managers who consider quality to be important.

I want to thank the many reviewers of my book for investing time and suggesting improvements: Ard-Jan Moerdijk, Ben Liu, Chris Spanner, Heidi Araya, Johan van Dongen, Martin Wiseman, Paul Hookham, Peter Rubarth, Piotr Jachimczak, Rene Ummels, Sharon Bockhoudt, Tom Gilb, Shiv Sivaguru, Srinath Ramakrishnan, Stephen Janaway, William R. Corcoran, and Vasilij Savin. Special thanks goes to Brandi Olson, Rik D'huyvetters, and Yanto Hesseling, for proofreading several versions of the book and providing many suggestions. Your feedback has helped me to make this a better book.

I feel honored having a foreword by Bill Curtis in which he emphasized how important quality is and confirms that quality assurance and speed of delivery can go together.

Finally, I would like to thank all the people who invest time to read my blog and comment on the posts. Your feedback helps me to increase my understanding of the topics that I write about and makes it worthwhile for me to keep blogging!

Ben Linders
September 2017

Introduction

This book views software quality from an engineering, management, and social perspective. It explores the interaction between all involved in delivering high-quality software to users and provides ideas to do it quicker and at lower costs.

What's in This Book

In this book, I explore how quality plays a role in all of the software development activities. It takes a deep dive into quality by listing the relevant factors of development and management activities that drive the quality of software products. It provides a lean approach to quality by analyzing the full development chain from customer requests to delivering products to users.

The book starts by explaining what Driving Quality is all about – introducing software quality and explaining why it matters.

The chapter Deep Dive into Quality explores the factors that drive quality in software activities performed by development teams and explains what managers can do to support teams of professionals in pursuing quality.

The chapter Quality Software with Agile Teams contains stories and case studies showing how the quality of software products can be improved. They are based on my experience working with teams and managers, helping them to face and solve quality issues, and improve their performance for sustainable and lasting results.

What Drives Quality doesn't intend to teach you the theory behind quality or provide detailed descriptions of all possible quality practices. The Bibliography provides an extensive list of books, articles, and links, that you can use to acquire in depth knowledge on software quality.

How To Use the Book

This is a practical book with many techniques and ideas that you can apply in your specific situation, within the method or framework that you are using. It aims to help you to improve the quality of the products that you deliver to your users.

There are many suggestions in this book, things which might help you to improve quality. They are marked as tips with a key symbol:

Try those tips that look suitable and see if they works for you. If they do, great! If not, try another one.

I also added many stories and cases from organizations that I have worked with to share my experience:

Stories and cases are boxed with a user symbol. Use them to get inspiration and think about what you might do to improve quality.

The suggestions provided in this book are suitable for agile teams and the management of agile organizations given the fact that many software development organizations have or are adopting agile. Specific agile quality practices are also described, with advice on how to apply them effectively based on an agile mindset.

Register your book today to get access to supporting materials at benlinders.com/what-drives-quality.

With plenty of ideas, suggestions, and practical cases on software quality, this book will help you to improve the quality of your software and to deliver high-quality products to your users and satisfy the needs of your customers and stakeholders.

Driving Quality

Many methods for product quality improvement start by investigating the problems and then working their way back to the point where the problem started. For instance audits and root cause analysis work this way. But what if you could prevent problems from happening, by building an understanding what drives quality, thus enabling you to take action before problems actually occur?

> Almost everyone that I have met in my career agrees that it's better to prevent defects or detect them earlier in software development than to have them found by the users of their products.

Still, many companies struggle with changing their process from "testing or inspecting quality in" to achieving quality from the start – through culture, design, craftsmanship, and leadership.

What is Quality

The quality of a software product or system is primarily how it satisfies the needs of the users, customers, and stakeholders, and delivers value to them. This definition takes an *external view*. It puts quality in the eyes of the beholders: the users, customers, and stakeholders decide if a software product or service has sufficient quality, or not.

> If the quality of a software product is insufficient according to the users then they will not use it. If the customers or stakeholders do not get enough value from the product, then they will not buy or support it. Satisfying the needs of all is crucial for software (or any) products to be successful.

How to Deliver Quality

Teams can only deliver quality if they are driven by the needs of the users, customers, and stakeholders. But how can you ensure that you are able to develop products that meet these needs? This is where an *internal view* of quality helps us. An internal view looks at the architecture and design of the software. It explores the processes and practices that are used to deliver the software. It focuses on the culture of the company, leadership, goals, and reward systems that drive the right behavior.

> Agile teams need to decide how they will develop and test their software. My experience working with agile teams tells me that having a solid Definition of Done (DoD) helps to know when products have sufficient quality. Successful teams stick to their agreed upon DoD and adapt it when it turns out that the delivered quality is insufficient. They are supported by their managers, who expect them to define, use, and improve their DoD, and allow them time to do this.

The internal quality view helps to develop software that is understandable and maintainable. Software that can easily be changed when there are new requirements or when the environment in which the software is used changes and the software needs to be adapted.

The Why of Quality

I see a lot of attention paid to the *How* of quality. We have dozens of models like ISO 9000 and ISO 25010, TQM, CMMI, People-CMM, Agile and Lean, and Kanban which tell us how we should develop software, and manage software development. We know how to do agile self-assessments, agile retrospectives, and root cause analysis to improve the way we work. We can even measure quality.

But do we understand and give enough attention to the *Why* of quality? Do we talk to the users of our products? Do we know what is important for them and why? Do we actually know our users? How do they use our software and what value do they want to get from using it?

Quality is in the eye of the beholder, so in the end, it are the users who judge if we are delivering quality or not, and what our product is worth. A good understanding of why quality is important and what our users consider quality to be is crucial to delivering high-quality software products.

Combining Why and How

To reach quality you need a good combination of understanding why and deciding how.

> To deliver quality you have to understand why a user needs certain functionality. Ask yourself why they want the system to be available 24/7? Find out why they want the software to be easy to use, and with fast response times? Why they need it next week, and not at the end of the year, what makes it so important for them?

Just knowing your user's needs (the requirements) is not enough, you must also understand why the users need it, what is it that they want to accomplish, what is important for them, what's the value? Only then can you deliver real quality!

Deciding how is about how you will develop and deliver a quality product or service.

You have to know how to deliver within budget and time constraints, with the professionals and the knowledge and skills that are currently available. And you must also decide what processes, practices, and tools you will use to develop the product, and manage teams, projects, or products.

Quality Practices

This book explores the role of quality in software development activities. It takes a deep dive into quality with the Quality Factors Model. This model lists the relevant quality factors of each development phase (a bunch of activities usually done at the same time). It describes why these factors drive the quality of products and how you can influence them.

Although the term "phase" is used, it doesn't mean that a specific sequence of activities is required to improve quality. The Quality Factors Model doesn't prescribe or assume any specific lifecycle.

Practices and suggestions which drive quality are provided which you can use to improve the quality of the products that you deliver to your users. They can be applied in waterfall or iterative projects that for example use Prince-2 or RUP, by agile teams using frameworks like Scrum, Kanban, or XP, and in organizations that are doing large scale agile software development with for instance the Scaled Agile Framework (SAFe), Large Scale Scrum(LeSS) Disciplined Agile Delivery (DAD), Nexus or Agility Path.

Deep Dive Into Quality

To build quality in from the start when developing software products, a deep understanding of what drives quality is essential. This chapter explores the Quality Factors Model, a detailed approach which explains the factors that drive quality in software development and management activities.

Researching Software Quality

As an affiliate of the Software Engineering Institute (SEI), I investigated factors that influence the quality of software products. I documented the results of my research in the report Building Process Improvement Business Cases Using Bayesian Belief Networks and Monte Carlo Simulation.

The aim of my research was to investigate high maturity measurement approaches that use limited but sufficient measurement effort to build a business case and gain management commitment and funding for quality improvement initiatives. This metric-based quality improvement approach is suited not only for high maturity organizations that already have data, but also for lower maturity organizations that are starting to deploy measurements and want to make sure that their quality improvements are driven by business value.

In my research, I modeled factors that could influence software quality to predict the quality of the products delivered by the organization. The original Quality Factors Model, which I developed when working at Ericsson, was defined based on research and industry reports and the combined experience of myself and the SEI in the areas of quality, measurement, and analysis.

The model contained both technical phases (e.g. requirements, design, implementation, test) and management activities (e.g. line

5

management, process management, project management). The model was reviewed by Ericsson employees, SEI researchers, and by international experts in the area of software quality.

Quality Factors Model

The Quality Factors Model that I initially developed was not intended to be generally applicable, I investigated those factors that were considered important for the organization that I was working with at that time. Over time the model has been revised and turned into a more generic model which is the one described in this chapter. My expectations are that many of the factors that drive quality in the current model will also be important for your organization.

The Quality Factors Model contains both technical phases with activities for developing software products and management activities which support software development.

The technical activities of the Quality Factors Model are organized into these technical phases:

- *Requirements* – Specify the products to be developed and supporting activities such as requirements clarifications, prioritization, commitment, and requirements management and traceability.
- *Architecture and Design* – Define and support the solution architecture (i.e. functionality) and the software architecture (i.e. structure of software and non-functional requirements), and the global and detailed designs prepared by development teams before writing the code.
- *Coding* – Create the software product, using a programming environment and/or code generation tools to write the code.
- *Review and Inspection* – Techniques to investigate and discuss code or documentation to improve quality.
- *Test* – Verifying and validating the product, for example using functional testing, system testing, integration testing up to and including release testing.

The management activities are divided into the following management roles:

- *Senior Management* – CxO level managers like the CEO, CIO, CTO, and COO.
- *Operational Management* – Line managers, both middle management and team/department managers which manage the employees, and are responsible for the daily operation of the organization.
- *Project Management* – Managers of projects and programs that include software development and delivery activities.

Note that if your organization has adopted agile (and doesn't have project managers anymore) then the activities mentioned for project managers are probably best done by other roles, for instance, by tech leads, team leaders, or Scrum masters.

The factors mentioned in the following chapters are not in any particular order. Depending on your situation and the context their importance will vary. There is no one right answer, just as there are no best practices, only good practices in context.

Requirements

With requirements, I mean activities for specifying the products to be developed and supporting activities such as requirements clarification, prioritization, commitment, and requirements management and traceability.

Irrespective of which development method (waterfall, iterative, agile, etc) is used, you need to create a common understanding and agreement between the product owner/manager and the development team to deliver the right products.

Factors that drive Requirements Quality are (in no particular order):

1. *Requirements Management Capability* – Skill and experience level of the professionals performing the requirements managing activities.
2. *Requirements Commitment* – Agreements between the product owner/manager the project managers and team members, where the project/teams commit what to deliver.
3. *Requirements Stability* – Inverse of the number of requirement changes over time. The fewer requirement changes you have, the higher requirements stability will be.
4. *Requirements Process Maturity* – The quality of the defined and baselined requirements processes and practices, including supporting materials such as training and document templates.
5. *Roadmap Quality* – Usability of the roadmap with respect to requirements management.
6. *Scope Stability* – Impact of major project changes related to the product roadmap, including stability of the products to be developed, development teams, projects, and major changes in team/project funding or product delivery dates.
7. *Root Cause Analysis* – Capability to learn from defects found during development. Analyzing defects, determining com-

mon causes related to processes, tools, development environment, capabilities, management, and organization, and defining actions to prevent them from recurring.

8. *Requirements Definition Capability* – The skill and experience level of the people performing requirements definition.

Let's take a look at some of these factors in more detail, to see how they drive quality.

Requirements Management Capability

To enable the delivery of products with sufficient quality, agile teams need to have user stories that are ready at the start of a sprint.

> Teams can use a Definition of Ready (DoR) to check the quality of the user stories. A DoR states the criteria that a user story should meet to be accepted into an iteration.

Some useful resources to make your own Definition of Ready are:

- The INVEST principle by Bill Wake.
- 10 Tips for writing good user stories by Roman Pichler.
- The book – User Stories Applied by Mike Cohn.
- The book – 50 quick ideas to improve your user stories by Gojko Adzic.
- Using a Definition of Ready on InfoQ.
- Exercise cards for defining your DoR and DoD by David Koontz.

Requirements Commitment

The purpose of requirement commitment is to have agreements between the stakeholders and projects/teams about delivering a product with specific functionality to the customers.

Agile teams use product backlogs to manage their requirements. Product owners prioritize the user stories. Waterfall and iterative projects usually define priorities up front in their project plans.

Having commitment on the requirements by all involved stakeholders is important as it ensures that you are developing a product that your customers need and are willing to pay for. Projects/teams also need to be committed to doing whatever they can to deliver products with the specified functionality.

> You don't need to have a commitment on everything for developing products. It is unfeasible, too expensive and takes too long to get.

Product owners/managers often have to decide with imperfect and incomplete information. In the book Product Mastery Geoff Watts suggests reducing the number of options, be clear about the criteria on which you need to decide, involve people in the decision, and accept that decisions cannot be perfect.

In order that teams can start developing products, you have to make sure that stakeholders agree on the priorities and that there is sufficient commitment to warrant investing time and money.

> My advice is to find out and verify what needs to be delivered first. I usually ask the stakeholders the question "What do we need now?"

Having prioritized user stories that are ready at the start of an iteration helps to increase commitment from the stakeholders and the development team, resulting in higher product quality.

> To be able to act upon changing requirements a good approach is to commit to as little as possible. Olav Maassen and Chris Matts suggest in their book Commitment to "never commit early unless you know why". This is a good approach to deal with change.

Requirements Stability

Requirements stability is the inverse of the number of requirement changes over time. The fewer requirement changes you have, the higher requirements stability will be.

The aim of requirements stability is not to prevent changes to requirements from happening – they will happen. Discouraging them or (even worse) ignoring them is no solution either.

It matters that projects and teams are sufficiently capable to deal with changes and can maintain stability during development.

> Developers and tester should use the available possibilities to ask for clarification if something is not clear with the requirements. Agile teams often do this during the sprint planning, product backlog refinement or backlog grooming meetings.

The purpose of product backlog refinement or backlog grooming meetings is to keep the backlog up to date and orderly. These meetings are also often used to discuss the business value and priority of the backlog items.

> My suggestion is to mark requirements which are insufficiently clear (except of course for the ones which are clarified during meetings) so that it is clear for product owners and team members that more work needs to be done before they can be pulled into an iteration.

Time and money are invested in an iteration. Every decision on adding a user story to the iteration backlog of a team is actually an investment decision – which is something many teams and organizations are not aware of.

Agile teams using Scrum treat requirements as being stable during an iteration (sprint). When a user story is added to an iteration the assumption is that there is a real need for software that fulfils the requirement described in the user story.

In agile, the requirements are fixed during an iteration and flexible over iterations (more on this in fixing scope in agile projects).

If there is a risk that a requirement underlying a user story may change at short notice then it may be better to select a different high priority user story for the next iteration.

> It's a good practice to always have user stories ready for 2-3 iterations so that it is possible to switch user stories during the sprint planning.

Having sufficient user stories ready also helps if teams finish all user stories before the end of an iteration. At that time they can agree with the product owner to pick another high priority user story and add it to the ongoing iteration.

Iterations can also be used to clarify requirements. You can use a spike, a practice from eXtreme Programming, to research a requirement or to investigate the feasibility of a technical solution which helps you to drive out risk and uncertainty.

This is somewhat similar to using a Minimum Viable Product (MVP) in Lean Startup to increase the knowledge of what users really need.

Roadmap Quality

Product roadmaps typically contain information about:

- When to develop which product versions.
- Business cases for product versions.
- Allocation of scope to versions.
- Product and feature introduction dates and plans.

- End of maintenance dates.
- Phase out dates.

The purpose of roadmaps is to synchronize and align activities of all involved. They should reflect current insights, which means that they will change frequently based on feedback from users, customers, stakeholders, and development teams.

It's important to keep roadmaps up to date and communicate changes to keep everyone involved. You may think that that's a no-brainer, but I've seen many organizations where only senior product managers worked with the roadmaps and didn't involve others – which is (literally) not a workable solution.

Transparency is essential if people want to work together effectively. My advice is to make roadmaps accessible for everyone and use them as information radiators.

Scope Stability

Many organizations struggle with changing requirements. The scope of their projects is unstable, which can have a major impact on the quality of the developed products.

Managing scope stability increases the quality and effectiveness of development projects.

One solution that is used in agile is to stabilize the requirements for an iteration. This helps teams to focus and deliver working software in small chunks.

Risk management techniques can be used to identify potential changes, and to take actions to limit impact, for instance by clarifying requirements or reducing the project scope before starting development.

Story mapping can be used to visualize the product that needs to be developed. It uses a matrix to horizontally group the functionality and vertically slice it up into iterations. Discussing the story map helps to discover missing functionality and to prioritize in which order the product will be delivered (most valuable parts first).

Requirements Definition

The requirements definition capability has to do with how you communicate requirements – ultimately the definition has to be in the head of the developers and testers.

Using a requirement specification document (or any other written format like use cases or even user stories in agile) often leads to confusion, resulting in developing wrong products that the users don't need.

In agile, the sprint planning is a meeting held at the start of an iteration where all involved discuss what needs to be developed. It's important is that assumptions made by the developers and testers are communicated and checked with those responsible for supplying the requirements. In agile, those are usually the product owners.

> It is essential to have frequent in-depth communication between development teams and the product owners or managers and (future) users about what the software should do to ensure that the right products are developed. Development teams should be able to ask for clarification if something is not clear. They should develop a good understanding of how the products will be used.

In agile, the ability to write effective user stories enables teams to deliver the right products fast. Effective user stories express the needs of users and support effective communication and collaboration between product owners and agile teams. They are prompts for communication which help to understand the needs of users and give clarity to ensure the right products are built.

> Richer communication techniques have proven to significantly reduce requirements ambiguity and improve clarity. Examples are face to face discussions, requirement clarification workshops, visiting users and involving them, and agile planning and backlog grooming. They serve to verify the requirements with product owners and users and help to map them to engineering tasks.

Defining the requirements may include activities like user experience (UX) design or user interface (UI) design. The aim of such activities is to help teams to produce a software product that is easy to use and does what users expect that it would do. Developers and testers need to communicate closely with the designers doing UX/UI activities to understand how the product should look and how the users will be using it.

Acceptance Test Driven Development (ATTD) is a practice where the acceptance criteria are discussed and acceptance test cases are defined before code is produced. It's primarily intended to increase the understanding of the requirements using different views: what do the users need, how can we solve that, and how can we test it.

> On many occasions, I've seen the value of having testers involved when defining and clarifying requirements. Their questions have often lead to a better understanding and earlier identification of flaws and risks.

Behavior Driven Development (BDD) is a practice to describe the required behavior of the software. Using conversations, concrete examples, and automated tests, it helps to streamline the communication between product owners/managers, domain experts, and teams about what the software should do. It can also be used to define acceptance criteria which can be automated as described earlier in ATTD.

Root Cause Analysis

Many defects found during reviews or in testing have their origins in the requirements activities. Root cause analysis is a practice for finding the deeper causes of such problems.

> I consider the ability to do root cause analysis to be an important driver for software quality. Major or frequently occurring defects often provide valuable information about flaws in your products and/or development processes, which you can use to improve the quality of your products.

For root cause analysis I prefer to use the Apollo method described in the book Apollo Root Cause Analysis by Dean L. Gano. Strong points of this methods are that it facts (not assumptions) and timing are taken into account when looking for cause-effect relationships.

Note: The above mentioned book is out of print. Dean's recent book RealityCharting provides a causal analysis process which can be used to visualize all causes, the interrelationships between causes, and effective solutions to prevent recurrence.

Increasing Requirements Quality

To deliver high-quality products to customers, quality practices have to be ingrained throughout development – quality starts with ensuring the quality of the requirements!

Architecture and Design

With architecture and design, I mean activities to define and support the solution architecture (i.e. functionality) and the software architecture (i.e. structure of software and non-functional requirements), and the global and detailed designs prepared by development teams before writing the code.

Factors that drive Architecture and Design Quality are (in no particular order):

1. *Architecture Stability & Flexibility* – The quality of the architecture definitions that are described in architecture documents and supported by architects.
2. *Analysis & Design Capability* – The skill and experience level of architects and designers. This includes capabilities for communication and cooperation between multiple teams involved in product development.
3. *Root Cause Analysis* – Capability to learn from defects and address their causes.
4. *Requirements Performance* – Result of the previous phase as described in Requirements.
5. *Project Management Performance* – Definition, planning, tracking, and control of quality in the projects.
6. *Process Management Performance* – Defining and baselining the processes to be used for architecture and design.
7. *Architecture & Design Process Maturity* – The quality of the defined and baselined architecture and design processes, including supporting material such as training and document templates.

Let's take a look at some of these factors in more detail, to see how they drive quality.

Architecture Stability and Flexibility

Architecture stability and flexibility is about a balance where you want an architecture to be stable (it is a foundation for the whole software product) but also flexible (to support future additions and enhancements).

Refactoring is a technique used to continuously restructure your code when the architecture or design changes. The purpose is to keep it maintainable. Refactoring should not change the external behavior of the product.

In most of the organizations that I work with, there are software architects assigned. They are responsible for the dependencies and interfaces in the software. Often they also define the "non-functional requirements" like performance, availability, and security.

Software architects should work intensively together with developers and testers in the teams to ensure stability and help them to implement new functionality. They should explain to teams why a specific architectural solution has been chosen.

Performance and Security

Where non-functional requirements like performance or security should be requested by product managers/owners, architects should come up with solutions to make them possible.

Architects and teams need to have a good understanding of how and where performance matters. They should have insight into things like the response times that users expect, how quickly their input should be processed, and how much time is allowed between clicking a button and providing a report or result.

Security requirements can be challenging, and implementing them often isn't easy. Too much security can make it difficult to use products, too little security poses risks of unauthorized and unwanted usage of the software.

The architecture should provide the means to develop software that performs fast enough. Spikes can be used to investigate potential solutions.

> Collaboration and communication between the architects, product managers/owners, and teams are key to deal with performance and security. My suggestion is to start discussions about this at the start of development so that architects can think about solutions that will make it possible, and prevent things that might block or hamper proper performance and security.

Architectural Practices

There are many useful practices that help you to increase your analysis & design capability.

> You can explore and demonstrate the feasibility of a possible architectural or design solution using a proof of concept. This is often done by implementing the solution in a small setting and in such a way that you can verify the usability. XP uses the term spike: "a very simple program to explore potential solutions".

> Design patterns are general reusable solutions to commonly occurring problems within a given context. Architects and developers should know many different design patterns and become experienced in applying them.

Root Cause Analysis

Root cause analysis is a practice for finding the deeper causes of such problems.

As an example, here's how I have led a root cause analysis session on a major product performance issue. The team had already tried several ways to reproduce and isolate the problem, but they weren't having success.

> In the root cause analysis session, we analyzed several cause-effect paths. For instance, we looked at a path starting from the effect that was visible at the customer's site and analyzed what software component(s) would cause such behavior. The analysis helped the software development team to investigate parts of the source code, and look for possible code fragments that could cause the performance issues. They also took a detailed look at the architecture to see where it helped or hindered performance and came up with ideas which could improve performance.

Together with the team I also investigated why the problem had not been found with system testing before the product was released:

> Several root causes were identified, which helped the team to setup a test which could capture the problem. It also helped them to improve system testing to prevent similar problems in the future. The team used results from the root cause analysis to improve the architecture and code, and extend system testing. It enabled them to reproduce the problem, implement a solution, and deliver a tested update to the customer. Exploring different cause-effect paths turned out to be a very effective approach to solve the problem.

More information about how to do effective root cause analysis can be found in the section on requirements.

Process Support and Coaching

Process management includes all activities that support professionals when applying processes, methods, and practices. This includes support in the operational usage of the processes for instance, with training, instructions, tools and document templates, and the availability of online process information and experienced coaches.

The amount of process support that is needed depends on the size and complexity of the products being developed and the type of products and the purpose for which they are used.

Big and complex products require more teams which need processes to work effectively together. They need to be trained to understand the processes and know how to use them to do their work.

Coaching is essential to make processes work – it helps people to apply them effectively in their specific situation.

A good coach will establish a relationship with people before problems start escalating and is available when problems might happen.

The way that people are coached can make a huge difference. It's not about the coaches, it's coaching and the coachees that matters most!

Coding

With coding, I mean activities to actually create the software product, using a programming environment or code generation to write the code.

Factors that drive Coding Quality are (in no particular order):

1. *Coding Environment* – The quality of the coding environment (e.g. supported functionality, stability, performance).
2. *Root Cause Analysis* – Capability to learn from defects found during development.
3. *Coding Capability* – The skill and experience level of the design teams with respect to coding and how to increase coding craftsmanship.
4. *Architecture & Design Performance* – Result from the previous phase as described in Architecture.
5. *Project Management Performance* – Definition, planning, tracking and control of quality in the development projects and the delivered products.
6. *Process Management Performance* – Defining and baselining the processes to be used for management activities and technical work.
7. *Design Base Quality* – Quality of the legacy product used as a design base for developing the new product or product version.
8. *Coding Process Maturity* – The quality of the defined and baselined coding processes, including all supporting materials such as training and code templates.

Let's take a look at some of these factors in more detail, to see how they drive quality.

Coding Environment and Tools

Much has been written about coding environments and the effect that they have on productivity and quality. Programmers want to have good tools to be able to do their work.

Coding tools should support collaboration, helping (distributed) teams to create and maintain code together. They should provide easy access to the code, and visualize it in such a way that programmers can easily read and understand a piece of code.

I see organizations that try to fully automate their coding rules, for instance with automatic code checking in their version control system. Any piece of code that does not comply to the rules will be rejected at check-in. Programmers often dislike this, as a result, it decreases productivity and often hampers quality. Programmers will look for ways to bypass the code checking system. They may be allowed to bypass it in times of pressure which opens the door for bad quality software.

It is better to train and coach programmers in writing good code than to use a tool that bashes them. Most coding rules also have exceptions, a good programmer knows when to apply a rule, and when not.

Spikes are a great way to deal with risks in projects as early as possible (see Architecture). Automated testing is indispensable to verify if the code is still ok after changes have been made (see Test).

Proper reuse of software can significantly improve the quality.

Open source code often has high quality, "given enough eyeballs, all bugs are shallow."

It is essential to only reuse code that has proved to have high quality, for instance, code that is working correctly in many applications, has gone through a good process that ensures quality, and that has been reviewed and tested extensively.

Code smells are symptoms in the code that possibly indicate a deeper problem. You don't know for sure if it will pose problems.

My advice is to do reviews or walkthroughs of code with colleagues. Working with teams showed me that it takes a lot of experience to recognize code smells and to know when and how to refactor code to improve the quality. You can develop your code smell skills by pairing or swarming.

Tools for static code analysis can help you to find software faults in an early stage (actually before the code is executed). There exist open source/non-commercial tools and commercial products for many different programming languages. These tools can discover read and write overflows, uninitialized memory, buffer underrun, unreferenced variables, overwrites, and incorrect API usage.

When I started writing programs I used tools like lint and QA-C to analyze my code. Initially, the tools gave an overload of information, especially on legacy code that has not been developed according to specific coding rules. I quickly learned how I could configure code analysis tools and how to read the reports that they generated to get useful information out of them.

It's essential to customize static code analysis tools using the organizational design and coding rules.

Continuous Integration (CI) is a practice where code that is changed is integrated frequently (for instance several times a day) in the repository. Check-ins are verified with automated builds and with automated regression tests. The biggest advantage is that integration issues are found quickly and can be resolved more easily.

An effective continuous integration process can help to reveal problems quickly. It's something that's worth to invest time and money in.

Continuous Deployment (CD) is an approach where software is deployed rapidly and safely, usually supported by tools. In case problems appear in production, a rollback can be done. CD enables teams to deliver fast and get user feedback quickly.

DevOps aims to increase end-to-end collaboration between DEVelopment and OPerationS. It's a combination of cultural philosophies, practices, and tools. DevOps builds upon agile and supports practices like CI and CD.

The book Continuous Delivery by Jez Humble and David Farley explains how you can deliver high-quality valuable software products in an efficient, fast, and reliable way. Their suggestion is to use frequent automated releases, remove error-prone manual tasks and shorten the feedback loop with users of the products.

The quality of the design base, the legacy code, directly influences the quality of the products since this code is a part of the products.

Knowing how to manage your technical debt, and when and how to improve quality of existing code, enables you to deliver high-quality products.

Application Performance Management (APM) can provide useful data about how systems are performing. You can use the data to improve your product as it provides information how users are using the systems and which parts are used and which not. You can also use APM data for continuous process improvement.

Craftsmanship

The manifesto for agile software development states: "Individuals and interactions over processes and tools". Focusing on software craftsmanship will deliver better quality.

There are several ways to increase your coding capabilities. A book by Bob Martin, The Clean Coder, gives examples of how programmers can exercise and sharpen their skills with coding dojos and doing katas. Another recommended reading on this topic is The Software Craftsman by Sandro Mancuso.

Join an open source project to learn from others and develop your programming skills.

Conferences where software developers can learn from other developers and practice their skills are xpdays, QCon, goto;, and JavaOne.

Debugging is a key skill to find bugs quickly and resolve them. In Effective Debugging, Diomidis Spinellis explains many useful debugging methods, strategies, techniques, and tools.

Test first approaches, the most well known being Test Driven Development (TDD), suggest to write automated tests before you write the production code. This will result in a test set that can be used for regression testing.

Initially, it will take extra time to write the test but you will gain time due to higher quality. The software will do exactly what is needed – nothing less but also nothing more.

The main benefit is that you will write just enough code (you stop writing code once the test passes) with higher quality (it's tested!). It also means less debugging, and it will be easier to refactor code.

> My experience is that it takes quite some discipline to do test first. This is not a practice that is suitable for every programmer!

The working environment and craftsmanship of your programmers can have a significant impact on the quality of your software products. Continuous code quality improvement is vital to prevent quality issues being reported by your users.

People and Processes

Regarding process management performance, I've deliberately used the term processes here although I know that lots of people are allergic to it. For me, a process is "the way we work around here". It shouldn't be a big document – the best processes are in the heads of people and not in their cabinet.

I consider the "Definition of Done" in agile to be a process. It is the way that teams agree to work together to deliver value.

> If teams do retrospectives and decide to do things differently in the future, those are process changes.

Some of the things that you can explore in retrospectives are:

- Do people know the processes and know how they are working together when they use them?
- Have they been trained in how to use them?
- Is there feedback from the actual usage?
- Are processes updated and good practices shared?
- Do we know the performance of our processes?

Review and Inspection

Reviews and inspections are techniques to investigate and discuss code or documentation to improve its quality.

Factors that drive Review and Inspection Quality are (in no particular order):

1. *Review and Inspection Policy and Strategy* – Describing the need for reviews and inspections and the expected benefits.
2. *Review and Inspection Process Performance* – Checks such as audits, retrospectives, or (self-)assessments to determine whether processes are effective and efficient.
3. *Review and Inspection Capability* – The skill and experience level of the people doing reviews and inspections.
4. *Review and Inspection Process Maturity* – The quality of the defined and baselined processes, including all supporting materials such as training and checklists.
5. *Coding performance* – Result from the previous phase as described in Coding.
6. *Project Management Performance* – Definition, planning, tracking, and control of quality in the development projects and the delivered products.

Let's take a look at some of these factors in more detail, to see how they drive quality.

Policy and Strategy

Policies for reviews and inspections should state the business benefits that are expected from doing them. The strategy describes which reviews and inspections are performed in the projects/teams and which kinds of defects are expected to be found in them.

Reviews and inspections can be done by finding defects, reporting and discussing them in a meeting, and having them removed by the author. This approach is called "cleanup mode".

Often it is more effective to sample code or documents, identify the quality by finding major defects, understand why those defects were inserted and use this knowledge to rewrite the code or documentation in such a way that those defects will not be made again. The focus for these kind of reviews is on learning and preventing defect, using root cause analysis.

Tom Gilb defines the term Specification Quality Control in his book Competitive Engineering as "systems engineering process control through sampling measurement of specification quality". The focus is on finding faults early, not to 'correct them' but to understand the defect density, and prevent exit when it is uneconomically high. Then also learning what causes recurrent-cause defects to prevent making similar mistakes in the future.

This process is described in Agile Specification Quality Control. The emphasis in the longer term than a given specification, is to drive inserted defects down, by teaching and reminding spec writers what the good practice rules are.

Software reviews and inspections significantly improve the quality of products, and provide major savings in cost and time. They provide significant business value if they are performed by skilled professionals guided by a policy and strategy.

Reviews and inspections can be documented in a test plan, project plan, or quality plan, thus becoming part of the verification and validation strategy for a product.

Agile teams usually use the DoD to define when and how reviews and inspections need to be done.

Remember that Quality Assurance is much more than testing, as described in the Real QA Manifesto – real benefits come from defect prevention, not from finding them!

I consider pair programming and mob programming to be variants of review. It's a kind of continuous real time review where faults and lower quality code pieces are spotted and corrected at the moment when they enter the software.

> My recommendation is to do pair or mob programming only for more complex pieces of code or when the risk of making mistakes is higher. My experience is that most programmers have a gut feeling when to do pair or mob programming and when not, which they can refine by analyzing defects that are found in reviews, during testing, or by users.

Pair working, a term coined by Yves Hanoulle, can be effective in many situations. You can use it to learn from each other and sharpen your skills.

I recall one time when I needed to correct records directly in a database, given that one of my programs had corrupted the content. It was tricky, as any mistake made during correction could further degrade the database.

> I paired with a colleague where I searched for the faults and corrected them and my colleague ensured that everything was still correct syntactically and semantically. He watched the screen and would halt me if anything might go wrong. It was a pretty intense two-hour session, but we managed to correct everything and keep the database and the system working properly.

Reviews and inspections help to continuously improve the quality of your code when applied in a sensible way. You can combine them with refactoring – reviews can help you to find the spots where refactoring is needed.

Process Adherence and Improvement

Just as any other process and practice, reviews and inspections can be improved by reflecting to find out what works well and what doesn't.

> When I was working as a quality manager, I usually attended the first couple of review meetings and do a short retrospective with the attendees. It helped them to become more effective in finding defects.

Mistakes that I see happening often in review meetings are: * Insufficient preparation. * Long (uncontrolled) discussions. * People slacking off during the meeting. * Attacking the author. * Attendees that feel the need to make remarks to show off and make themselves look important.

> When you start with reviews I suggest assigning a coach that attends meetings and provides feedback at the end of each session to continuously improve review skills. Addressing and discussing mistakes with the attendees, with feedback on what actually happened during the meeting, helps them to learn and improve quickly.

Here's an example that shows how I dealt with a review meeting where people turned up being unprepared:

At one time, I was asked to moderate a formal review meeting of an architecture document. When starting the meeting, I asked the attendees if they had prepared for the meeting, by going through the document and making a list of the defects that they had found. Several attendees explained that they had not been able to prepare for the review, so I cancelled the meeting. I asked the attendees that had prepared to share their findings with the author in an informal way. A new date was set and the attendees committed that they would prepare themselves and sent in their remarks before the meeting.

Cancelling the meeting drew the project manager's attention. Shortly after the meeting he asked me into his office:

At first, he was quite annoyed as he had never seen any review cancelled before and didn't expect this behavior from his quality manager (it was my first day at the job!). When I explained the risks of having the review done with insufficient preparation, he changed his mind and complimented me on taking this decision. He explained that it had happened more than once that significant problems turned up late in his projects, which gave major disturbances and delays to delivery dates. After listening to me, it became clear to him that by having well-prepared reviews those problems could have been prevented. He certainly didn't want this to happen to his projects anymore.

At the new review meeting, everybody was well prepared. The meeting took less time than usual, and there were several findings that would have turned into major problems later in the project if they had not been discovered by the reviewers.

Review and Inspection Capability

Various techniques exist to improve the effectiveness and efficiency of reviews and inspections.

Examples are:

- Focused reviews, for example, perspective-based reviews, role based reviews, and partial reviews by dividing the document among the reviewers.
- Collection of remarks before the review meeting, and distribution of all combined remarks to the reviewers.
- Design and coding rules (rule based reviews) – this can be combined with static code analysis.
- Statistical and/or Six Sigma techniques, like sampling, capture-recapture, and preparation time versus defect density.
- Focused reviews on maintainability issues, such as duplicated code, poor naming conventions, or code that is insufficiently covered by test cases.
- Specification Quality Control (described earlier in this section).

Moderators have a crucial role in the review meetings. By focusing on the process and culture they ensure that minimum time needs to be invested by the professionals to get maximum results.

Much time can be saved by selecting which defects need to be discussed in the review meeting, and which ones can be corrected directly by the author without further discussion. This is something that moderators should facilitate before and during the review meeting. Of course, the author can always contact the reviewer if (s)he needs more information after the meeting.

Moderators can explain and emphasize coding rules during the review meeting when they discover that rules have not been followed (which often happens because programmers didn't understand them).

> I have seen great results with moderators who analyzed major defects with the reviewers during the meetings, explored the causes, and provided suggestions to prevent similar defects in the future.

Reviews and inspections are effective techniques to increase the quality of your products, and find defects earlier at lower costs. They can also be used to convey knowledge about the software within the team and to learn and improve developer skills.

Test

Testing covers many ways of verifying and validating the product.
Factors that drive Testing Quality are (in no particular order):

1. *Test Strategy* – The strategy that describes how the test activities are organized and which kinds of defects are expected to be found by them.
2. *Test Capability* – The skill and experience level of the people doing the testing.
3. *Test Process Maturity* – The quality of the defined processes, including all supporting material such as training and test templates.
4. *Test Environment* – The quality of the test environment (e.g. tools and supported functionality, stability, performance).
5. *Platform Quality* – The functionality and stability of the product platform (e.g. operating system, middleware, support libraries, etc).
6. *Requirements Performance* – Result of the previous phase as described in Requirements.
7. *Coding (review) Performance* – Result from the previous phase as described in Coding.
8. *Project Management Performance* – Definition, planning, tracking, and control of quality in the development projects and the delivered products.
9. *Test Process Performance* – Checks such as audits, retrospectives, or (self-)assessments to determine whether processes are effective and efficient.

There is a lot published on testing, I guess it's number 1 in Quality Assurance (QA) with respect to publications, conferences, and professional networks. However, QA is not testing, and many of the defects that are found in testing could have been found earlier in a more economical way.

Testing can consume a large part of the project costs and time, so it is important to ensure that it contributes towards delivering higher quality. Knowing the factors that drive how testing influences quality can help you to get maximum business value out of your testing activities.

Let's take a look at some of these factors in more detail, to see how they drive quality.

Test Strategy

There's a significant difference between testing in waterfall projects and agile testing.

In waterfall projects testing is done in consecutive phases. It often starts with unit or functional testing, followed by system testing, integration testing up to and including release or end-to-end testing. Many organizations define their own specific testing phases.

> The main difference when agile is used is that testing activities are integrated with the development activities in the sprint/iteration. The purpose is to deliver a tested product which can be shipped to users at the end of the iteration.

Compared to waterfall similar test activities are done in agile, but only on the software that has been developed or may have been impacted in the iteration.

> If you want to learn about agile testing then I recommend to read More Agile Testing by Janet Gregory and Lisa Crispin.

In agile "release sprints" or "hardening sprints" can be used to prepare a product so that it can be released to the users. In such an iteration no new features are developed, in stead teams focus on catching up on testing activities and reducing technical debt.

My opinion is that you shouldn't plan hardening sprints up front, as it gives a signal that it's ok to deliver lower quality in your iterations and clean up later.

The Definition of Done should make clear to everyone involved that at all times the quality at the end of every iteration should be sufficient to release the software to the users.

Hardening sprints can be used at times when too much technical debt has been accumulated – then they can be an efficient and effective approach to deal with problems before adding new functionality.

How Many Defects do You Expect to Find

Defining a good test strategy and making test plans is crucial to deliver quality products. I see many test plans which describe the test phases, activities performed, and the test environment and test resources, which is a good foundation for effective testing.

From a quality point of view I want to see what kind of defects (and if possible how many defects) the teams expect to find in testing, but very few plans contain this and most teams don't have this insight. Still I consider this to be very important – allow me to explain why.

Having an idea of how many defects you will find helps you to build a business case for testing. If you expect to find many defects, then there might be good reasons to do testing, unless you can find those defects in a cheaper way, like using reviews or inspections. You might also think about defect prevention. Defining a business case will help to arrange sufficient time and money to do proper testing.

If the number and severity of the defects is expected to be low, then the question arises as to how much testing should be done? You might be able to do less testing and save time and money.

> To get insight into the quality of the product during development I suggest to measure two things: Defects introduced and defects detected.

Introducing defects happens during specification, architecture, design and coding – defects are either introduced into documents or into the actual product. Detection of defects is normally done in reviews/inspections and test.

> By using these two measurements you can determine if there is a quality risk, and what the origin is: Too many defects in the product and/or insufficient reviews or testing to capture the defects.

More information about this approach can be found in my conference paper Controlling Project Performance by Using the Project Defect Model and in the article Measuring and controlling product quality.

Most testers that I work with have some heuristics on the amount of defects that they expect to find with their tests. The defect management systems that they use often have data on this. It's programmers who often have no clue how many defects they have put in, simply because they don't maintain or analyze defect data.

> Programmers can gather data by simply logging or classifying where/when the defect was introduced in the defect management system. The data can be analyzed to find common causes.

Risk based testing suggest to only test those parts of the software that probably contain faults, and skip other parts in testing. To do it properly you need some idea on how many faults are there in the code, and how you expect to find them.

> Stating expectations on defects, and discussing them will help you to manage product risks and quality. You can make profound decisions on how much testing is needed, what testing should focus on, and when you can stop testing.

Having quantified your expectations on defects that testing should find makes it possible to measure how your testing activities are performing. If you are finding more defects, then the quality of the product may be lower than expected – which is something that you should investigate.

Be careful how you measure the cost of defects. In a book from Capers Jones on The Economics of Software Quality he explains very clearly how measuring costs of defects per testing phase can give the idea that the less defects you find (and thus the higher the quality of your product), the more expensive testing would become. I agree with him that this "cost of defect" measurement is wrong, and it also doesn't help you to take better decisions on what to test, where to test, and when.

> The two best approaches to measuring quality and testing that I have used are Cost of Quality (CoQ) and Total Cost of Ownership (TCO). These approaches provide a good insight into the losses due to bad quality and can help you to build a business case to improve quality.

Discussing the expectations from testing with developers in an early stage can save time and money. I have used a Project Defect Model to plan and track quality. This model supported discussions between developers and testers on the expected quality and helped them focus the test activities to find defects as early as possible. The benefits are clear: Fewer disturbances on the project, better able to deliver on time, and lower maintenance costs. And, most importantly – happier users. It also leaves your employees less frustrated.

Automated Testing

You need a mechanism to test existing functionality when new features are added or existing features are changed.

Given the rate of change, it can be beneficial to automate testing.

Automating testing can be done in several ways:

- Executable specifications, for instance using Behavior Driven Development (BDD) with a tool like Cucumber.
- Test First or Test Driven Development (TDD) using a test framework.
- Automated acceptance test.

Many teams try to automate far too much existing test functionality. My advice is to use a risk based approach for deciding what to automate to prevent spending too much time maintaining and debugging test automation.

In The Digital Quality Handbook Eran Kinsbruner explores how to ensure quality with mobile products. He advises to be careful on when to automate and when not: "Selecting the wrong test to be part of an automation suite could turn out to be very problematic and time-consuming."

Learn from Defects and Prevent Them

Root cause analysis helps to analyze defects that have slipped through testing, and to define and implement improvements to prevent similar defects slipping through in the future. Root cause analysis can also provide insight into the preceding activities, i.e. Requirements, Architecture and Design and Coding, thus providing opportunities to improve across the full product development lifecycle in a lean way.

The Capability Maturity Model Integration (CMMI) positions Root Cause Analysis at level 5, in the process area Causal Analysis and Resolution (CAR).

> Since in most organizations there are often (too) many problems that could be investigated, some kind of policy is needed to decide which ones to explore. The reason for investigating problems is to come up with effective actions for preventing similar problems in the future. Don't investigate problems that rarely happen or have low impact.

I use these criteria to decide which problems should be investigated:

- Major defects from test or customers.
- Significant disturbances with major impact.
- Frequently recurring problems.

If the problem fits with at least one of the three criteria, then you should do a root cause analysis. If not, then save your time and money for other problems to analyze.

CMMI V1.3 has extended the possibilities to do Root Cause Analysis at lower maturity levels, recognizing the business benefits that they can bring.

Testing Processes

Mentioning test process performance as a factor in testing quality may look surprising. My experience is that testing processes (the combination of all testing stages, test techniques, test environments, etc) can become very complex and are often difficult to manage.

> Taking a process view to testing, by analyzing test data and process performance, can help you to continuously improve your testing strategy and activities, resulting in higher quality at lower costs.

There has been, and still is, much debate on the need for processes with more and more organizations implementing agile. But remember my definition of a process, which is "the way we work around here". There's always a process.

> Agile teams also have processes – just look at the Definition of Done.

Agile actually has process management built in, by using retrospectives to evaluate and learn, and the sprint planning to tailor the process towards the needs of the current sprint. Process management hasn't disappeared in agile development – agile does it cheaper and often more effective!

Senior Management

With Senior Management, I mean the CxO level managers. It can be the CEO when quality is considered a top priority for the organization, or the COO when quality is crucial to delivering products and services. In IT companies it can be the CIO who drives IT quality, or the CTO when quality is considered as a technological advantage.

Factors that drive Quality by Senior Management are (in no particular order):

1. *Quality Commitment* – The amount time and money management is willing to personally invest in quality.
2. *Quality Reward Policy* – When and how employees are rewarded for their quality-related behavior and results.
3. *Leadership Capability* – The capability of senior managers to affect the organization's quality mission.
4. *Quality Culture* – A culture that enables people to strive for quality.
5. *Quality Goals* – Visible goals that show how quality delivers business value.

Let's take a look at some of these factors in more detail, to see how they drive quality.

Quality Commitment

Committed to quality, in my opinion, means that senior managers invest personal time and money in quality. It is much more about what is being done by managers than about what is said.

My experience is that showing up and doing it is what counts. Managers should walk the talk!

In an organization that I worked with I established a network of quality professionals. There were regular sessions to exchange experiences from applying quality methods and techniques:

> In one session we held a brainstorm to find out what could be done to improve quality. We used the EFQM Excellence model to organize our thoughts and found out that many of them were related to the EFQM strategy criteria. So the question arose how to deal with that?

When I discussed the quality network with senior managers of the company, they became enthusiastic and asked if they could join the next session to discuss their perspectives and to hear from their professionals.

> In the session there was an open discussion, where senior managers shared their concerns on quality, described how they saw the business value of quality, and explained their strategy to improve quality. They listened to the quality professionals, appreciated what they do to improve quality, and recognized how their day-to-day activities related to strategic goals.

The session was highly valued, both by the professionals and by the managers:

Reactions I got from the quality professionals are that this was the first time that managers really listened and understood what they do. Also they felt that management was committed to quality, a feeling that they hadn't got from the previous management presentations, newsletters, and blogging by managers. Having the managers in their network meeting, listening to them, and working together to come up with solutions to improve quality, really motivated them, and gave them energy to continue their quality journey.

Also the managers were impressed by the commitment of the quality professionals to support their customers, finding practical short-term solutions, and focus on continuous quality improvement. They recognized the value of the quality network, and decided that this network would remain connected with the senior management team, so that initiatives from the network could contribute to and benefit from company-wide quality improvements.

Agile teams use product reviews (called sprint reviews in Scrum) to demonstrate the software product and get feedback. Senior managers can show commitment by attending these meetings, participate in the discussions, and give feedback to the teams.

It is important to leave the teams in charge of the product reviews – don't try to gain control or micromanage the teams!

Leadership

Managers are expected to make things happen. To ensure quality it should be driven by managers. However, the way that they do this can make a huge difference.

Senior managers have to give the example when it comes to quality. They have to show that they care, not by saying but by doing – what people do tells more than what they say!

Things that managers can do to drive quality are:

- Give focus to quality, make it a top priority.
- Invest personal time in quality.
- Show that quality matters by showing up when there's anything quality related in the organization.
- Ensure that they have insight into the operation and the quality that it delivers.
- Make quality measurable: Set targets and follow up on the performance.
- Reward professionals that contribute to quality.

We need to move away from leadership approaches that are based on "command and control" to increase agility – and become faster and more flexible.

Innovative leadership approaches that I suggest to explore and practice are:

- Intent-based leadership.
- Holacracy.
- Sociocracy and Sociocracy 3.0.
- Reinventing organizations.
- Management 3.0 and Managing for Happiness.

Jurgen Appelo, a leadership expert, stated in his book Managing for Happiness that "Management is Too Important to Leave to the Managers". I fully agree with this. Organization that adopt agile should encourage management and leadership to take place at all levels by everyone.

For example, Scrum masters have to know and be able to apply effective leadership styles to serve agile teams.

Quality Culture

Setting the right culture for quality isn't easy. Many see the culture as a "soft thing", but a quality culture can bring "hard" benefits.

In Total Quality Management (TQM), Deming provides 14 points for management which help to establish a quality culture.

Agile software development emphasizes the need to develop a culture which empowers professionals and enables them to decide themselves how to develop high-quality software.

The People-CMM has several process areas that describe practices for culture change.

The American Society for Quality (ASQ) has a list with resources on culture of quality.

Many organizations use quality checklists, for instance at hand-overs or at quality gates. Since a checklist consists of short sentences or a single word, it only works when people using a checklist have sufficient knowledge about what they are checking.

> Somebody who is not trained and experienced enough cannot use a checklist, because even with a checklist (s)he wouldn't know what to look for and how to check it.

In the book Adrenaline Junkies and Template Zombies: Understanding Patterns of Project Behavior, such checking is called false quality gates. It isn't valuable, in fact it's a waste of time and money, and it demotivates people.

I am convinced that IT professionals want to do their work in a good way, and deliver quality products. Implementing a quality culture is often about removing barriers that hinder quality, breaking down walls that hinder collaboration, and giving professionals room to do their work in a good way.

Many organizations are unaware of how they discourage quality with their structure and rules, and when they understand it, it seems that they are unable to remove such overhead that hinders quality. You can observe a lot by just watching, if you know when, where and how to look!

Quality Goals

Balanced Scorecards are used in many organizations to define their goals and steer the operation. You can use them to set quality targets, and to oversee and manage the relationships between quality targets and other targets.

Scorecards enable communicating, measuring and analyzing quality targets, and they support defining corrective actions and following them to completion.

The scorecard targets need to be well defined with metrics that provide insight in the operation. My advice is to limit the number of targets and ensure that you understand the relationships between the targets in order to properly balance them – you can never reach all of them.

Methods like Lean Six Sigma can support you to measure the quality of your products and processes and continuously reduce waste.

Measurements help you to make quality improvement visible which stimulates continuous improvement.

Senior managers are usually interested in risks. Poor quality raises risk, so instead of talking about quality you may want to show your managers the effects that poor quality may cause. This can help you to get them involved and get support for activities that will improve quality and reduce risks.

Driving Quality

Senior Management can drive quality. Many failed quality improvement initiatives state that lack of commitment was one of the main root causes.

This section showed that management can show their commitment to quality by collaborating with the quality professionals in their company. By recognizing and rewarding quality and showing leadership they can set the right culture that drives professionals to deliver products which meet their quality goals, on time and within budget.

Operational Management

With Operational Management, I mean the line managers in organizations, both middle managers and team/department managers (not the Senior Managers). They are the ones who manage the employees of the organization and are responsible for the daily operation.

Factors that drive Quality by Operational Management are (in no particular order):

1. *Resource Capability Management* – Ability to improve and sustain improvements in the skills of employees, both technical skills and interpersonal (e.g. collaboration, communication, and feedback).
2. *Resource Allocation* – Allocation of developers, testers, and support staff to projects/teams.
3. *Resource Stability* – The same people remain on projects/teams for longer periods instead of being replaced.
4. *Schedule Pressure* – The way deadlines are used to put pressure on people to deliver on time can hamper quality.
5. *Operational Overview and Insight* – Insight into the status of ongoing projects (e.g. processes used, documents delivered, quality of the documents).
6. *Decision Making Capability* – The ability to balance quality, time, cost, and functionality, and to make decisions involving the right people.

Operational Management can drive quality by establishing a capable, stable workforce, which can deliver quality products and services in an efficient way, and by taking and communicating timely decisions so that professionals know what is expected from them.

Let's take a look at some of these factors in more detail, to see how they drive quality.

Capable Employees

The quality of the products and services that organizations deliver are strongly related to the capabilities, competence, and motivation of their employees. Operational Management is responsible for the development of their people.

> Managers need to ensure that their employees are capable to do their work in a good way, are motivated, and feel happy.

The People CMM contains practices for training and development and competency management, to ensure an empowered professional workforce.

Several authors have emphasized the need for training and practice development in software, like William E. Perry in his book iTeam: Putting the 'I' back into team (see also skills are crucial for a team to be successful) and Bob Martin in The Clean Coder.

Stable Teams

Results come from people that work together. They collaboratively design, develop and test the software. Relationships need to be established between professionals to work together in a productive way.

> Operational managers need to establish and maintain stable teams. They can do this for instance by arranging the work in packages that can be taken up by multidisciplinary empowered teams. They can also work on establishing a culture where people collaborate and support each other, both in and between teams.

Similar to keeping teams stable it is important to limit employee changes in key roles, like project managers, test managers, or technical leads/architects. Also you have to allow them slack time to assure they are available to the teams and the customers and stakeholders of the project. That will enable them to act quickly when needed, and to ensure that teams do not waste time, for instance due to waiting for decisions that need to be taken.

Effective Decisions

Part of any management role is the responsibility to take decisions and having the power to take them.

Operational managers often have to decide about who will be assigned to projects or teams, where teams will be doing their work, and about the possibilities for training or skill development. Professionals depend on these decisions, it is important for them that decisions are being made on time and that they are clearly communicated.

The CMMI has a process area called Decision Analysis and Resolution (DAR), that describes how criteria can be established and solutions identified and evaluated to take effective decisions.

I've used the Decision Analysis and Resolution process area in a CMMI Class C assessment with a management team of an R&D organization. This assessment gave them insight in how they were making decisions and gave them ideas for improving their decision making capabilities.

Data and facts can help managers to decide better. My advice is to start with deciding what should be measured. Some things are easy to measure, like time, money and defects. They seem to be ideal candidates to quantify what's being done in the organization: We all spend time and money on the work that we do, and we all find and solve defects. But that doesn't mean that those are the (only) things that should be measured.

> Not everything that can be counted, counts. Start from the mission or goal that you are trying to reach, agree upon what is relevant and important, and then define metrics, start measuring, and use the data to decide.

Together with Senior Management and Project Management, Operational Management drives professionals to deliver products which meet their quality goals, on time and within budget.

Project Management

With project management, I mean managing of projects and programs that include software development and delivery. This can be waterfall projects, iterative projects (e.g. using RUP or DSDM), or agile projects – the basic principles of project management and their contributions towards software quality are relevant for all of these kinds of projects.

Factors that drive Quality by Project Management are (in no particular order):

1. *Decision Making Capability* – The ability to balance quality, time, cost, and functionality, and to make timely decisions that involve the right people.
2. *Project Portfolio Management* – Planning and tracking of projects, including project steering groups and all decisions made to start, continue, cancel, and conclude projects.
3. *Project Management Capability* – Skill and experience level of project managers.
4. *Risk Management Process Capability* – Awareness of project risks, the maturity of the process, and the capability of managing risks.
5. *Planning Capability* – The ability to estimate, plan, and track projects with respect to the quality of the delivered product.
6. *Scope Stability* – Impact of major changes in the projects (e.g. those related to stability of the products to be developed), the development teams involved in the projects, and major changes in project funding or delivery dates.
7. *Schedule Pressure* – The way deadlines are used to put pressure on people to deliver on time can hamper quality.
8. *Operational Overview and Insight* – Insight into the status of ongoing projects (e.g. processes used, documents delivered, quality of the documents).

9. *Project Management Process Performance* – Checks such as audits, retrospectives, or (self-)assessments to determine whether processes are effective and efficient.

Project Management can drive quality by taking decisions that enable the project team to develop software. It should establish a structure and environment where teams can deliver quality products and services in an efficient way, and by taking and communicating decisions timely so that professionals know what has been agreed with the project stakeholders.

Let's take a look at some of these factors in more detail, to see how they drive quality.

Decision Making Capability

Project Managers are expected to take decisions or ensure that decisions are properly taken that are needed for projects to deliver and meet their goals.

> Product owners and teams should reach agreement about the product quality that is required and feasible. I consider their collaboration to be essential, since quality can have significant impact on the amount of work that needs to be done – impacting scope, functionality and delivery speed.

Depending on the project management method(s) that are used and how projects are steered and monitored, there can be big differences in which decisions are taken by project manager, and which are taken by members of the project team, or by stakeholders.

> In waterfall projects where project managers are responsible for planning the work they normally make decisions about what needs to be done, when to do it, who should do it, and maybe even how to do it.

In agile projects, the content of each iteration is usually decided in the sprint planning meetings. The product owners and teams discuss the user stories, estimate the work involved, and decide which stories will be included in the iteration.

Frameworks for Managing Projects

Project managers can use specific project management frameworks and methods, for example PRINCE2, PMI or IPMA. All of these frameworks provide a number of quality activities that are mandatory and others that are optional.

To use project management frameworks effectively they have to be tailored toward the needs of the projects and the organization. This requires in-depth knowledge of project management principles and practices described in the frameworks.

The CMMI includes process areas that cover project management and the quality activities that are typically performed on projects.

You can use CMMI process areas to assess your project management performance and find ways to improve the way that you are managing your projects.

Risk Management

The quality of the software products is related to how risks are managed in projects. Product quality risks should be identified early and continuously, and actions need to be taken to either reduce the chance that the risk occurs, or mitigate quality impact.

In agile, user stories that pose a high risk are usually done as early as possible.

It is better to do things with a higher risk early when there is more room to deal with the impact that they have. Spikes are a great way to deal with risks as early as possible. They decrease the chance of disturbances happening late and help agile teams and product owners to get quick feedback about solutions.

To reduce risk and improve quality, agile teams should develop their capabilities to deliver high-quality products. The section on coding provides suggestions how to do this.

Schedule Pressure

Several good books have been written on managing time and people on projects, two that I highly recommend are The Mythical Man Month from Fred Brooks and Peopleware from Tom DeMarco and Tim Lister. They make it very clear that (project and line) managers should carefully manage teams, and prevent professionals from being overloaded with work.

Also XP promotes a core practice "40 hour workweek" which aims to reduce pressure on team members and prevents making mistakes that would result in low quality.

My experience is that keeping team composition stable enables team members to learn and improve continuously.

Why do project managers put time pressure on their teams? I don't know why, and it still surprises me, so I can only guess at their reasons for doing it:

Maybe because they think that putting pressure on people makes them more productive? Or maybe that teams need deadlines to deliver results? They might see it as bargaining, where they want to find the optimum amount of work to be delivered within a time frame? It might be because their boss is putting pressure on them?

Project managers should remove distractions and interruptions from their teams, and establish an environment where people are not disturbed and can do their work effectively. In agile such things are normally done by Scrum masters – acting as servant leaders for the teams.

Be aware that there's a balance between shielding team members and enabling them to talk to customers and stakeholders to understand their needs. When in doubt don't block communication!

Summing up, there are lots of good reasons for project managers to reduce schedule pressure in order to reduce quality risks while developing products. The fact that so many managers still put pressure on teams surprises me.

Agile Project Management

Do we still need project managers to manage projects with agile teams? Yes we do, but their role will be different.

Project managers can for instance organize the coordination between agile teams in a project, for example with a Scrum-of-Scrums, to ensure that the subproducts delivered by the teams can be integrated and delivered to the users.

In larger projects they might do the delivery planning, to ensure that project deliveries are aligned with product roadmaps. They also have to align projects with all the customers and stakeholders, like project sponsors, line managers, and product managers, where this is not done by the product owners.

It also depends on the size of the organization and complexity of the problems that needs to be solved. A startup with one team doesn't need a project manager – a good tech lead or Scrum master should be enough. In a large organization with multiple products and services, the work of teams needs to be coordinated and aligned which warrants to have project, program, or product managers.

In the end, a project manager is responsible for steering product quality in agile teams and for the reporting of his/her agile project. Note that this requires close cooperation between project managers and Scrum masters and product owners, as together they are the ones who are driving quality in the daily activities of the teams.

My opinion is that there is still a need for project managers in agile, where they support the primary planning mechanisms from agile methods like Scrum.

Together with Senior Management and Operational Management, Project Management drives professionals to deliver high-quality products, on time, and within budget.

Quality Software with Agile Teams

Agile teamwork has shown to be a great approach to deliver high-quality software products. The agile values favor quality, and there are lots of agile practices available that teams can apply to develop high-quality software. Users are happy with the early and frequent deliveries of working software by those agile teams.

What is Software Quality?

I define high-quality software as "software that satisfies the needs of the users and delivers value to them." Quality is in the eye of the beholder – it are the users who decide if a software product or service has is quality, not the agile teams. Software has to be "fit for purpose" – user needs to be able to do their work using the software.

Teams can only deliver quality if they are driven by the needs of the users. In agile, this is supported by the agile values, and by intense collaboration between the product owners and the agile teams.

Agile Values Support Quality

The manifesto for agile software development describes the values that agile methods consider important. In my opinion, these values support the delivery of quality software:

- Individuals and interactions over processes and tools.
- Working software over comprehensive documentation.
- Customer collaboration over contract negotiation.
- Responding to change over following a plan.

Some examples how the agile values support quality are:

Working software over comprehensive documenta-tion focuses on delivering products to users. It en-courages early and frequent delivery, enabling users to use the software and start getting value.

Responding to change over following a plan results in higher quality, as it urges agile teams to adapt software that does not satisfy the needs of the users.

It is no surprise that agile teams deliver high-quality software and services to their users:

There's data on the business benefits of agile that confirms that agile supports quality. The State of Ag-ile Report from VersionOne also mentions enhancing quality as one of the main reasons why organizations adopt agile.

Stories on Agile Quality

This chapter – Quality Software with Agile Teams – explores how agile principles and practices can be applied to deliver high-quality software. It contains stories and case studies from my experience in working with teams and managers, helping them to face and solve quality issues, and improving their performance for sustainable and lasting results.

Agile provides significant benefits when it comes to quality. If you want to improve quality then it helps to make a business case for quality with agile.

As Philip Crosby stated years ago: quality is still free. But you need to have a quality mindset to delight your customers, and you will have to sell quality to your managers by showing them how it makes the business successful.

Agile quality practices like sprint planning meetings, daily stands-ups and retrospectives, and technical practices like pair programming or Test Driven Development all support the delivery of quality software.

Let's explore what happens when quality problems arise in software in a culture where people don't dare to speak up, being afraid to get punished if their managers finds out that their software isn't working properly: What if we fail?

Teamwork enables agile teams to deliver high-quality software; it enables them to decide how to do their work, and helps to continuously learn and improve their way of working.

Agile supports empowering teams, which is a more effective and quicker solution than adding people when quality becomes a problem. Empowered teams have what it takes to increase the quality of products.

Agile promotes that teams work in a sustainable pace, delivering value to their customers. When teams are working under too much pressure, technical debt will increase and velocity of teams will go down.

Teams can increase the quality of software with visual management. Making things visible helps teams to deliver products that their customers need and collaborate effectively with their customers and stakeholders.

Maintaining software programs costs lot of time and money, which organizations would like to invest in developing new functionality that brings value to their customers. You can reduce software maintenance by throwing your bad software code away.

Measuring defects can provide you with valuable information about the quality of your product, provided that you dive deeper to have a good understanding of the data and then act upon that.

Agile retrospectives can be used to investigate quality issues or to agree upon actions that can improve the quality of the software that is delivered.

Root cause analysis can be used in software development to build a shared understanding of a problem to determine the first or "root" causes. Knowing these causes helps to identify effective improvement actions to prevent similar problems in the future.

The stories in this chapter are meant to inspire you and give you ideas and energy to improve quality in your organization.

The stories also show how the practices described in Deep Dive into Quality have been used to deliver high-quality software.

Agile teams are driven by values that favor quality. They collaborate intensively with the users of the software and use practices to develop high-quality software products.

Business Case for Quality with Agile

Over the years there have been several investigations into the business benefits of agile. Several of them include how agile affects quality.

Donald J. Reifer stated in Six Agile Method Take Aways from the Reifer 2014 Quantitative Analysis of Agile Methods Study that "Agile quality, as measured in terms of defect densities post-release, averages about 6 percent better than that being experienced on plan-driven projects."

In his recent article Quantitative Analysis of Agile Methods Study (2017): Twelve Major Findings he stated that you can "expect agile software quality to exceed traditional method performance by a factor of from 6 to 12 percent in about three years."

Capers Jones stated in Evaluating Agile and Scrum with Other Software Methodologies that "When the focus of the evaluation turns to quality rather than speed, TSP, CMMI 5, and RUP are on top, followed by XP. Agile is not strong on quality so it is only number 8 out of 10."

In The Business Value of Using Agile Project Management for New Products and Services David Rico provides data on quality improvements from agile when compared to waterfall projects: 74% vs 50%, a 24% increase. In his book The Business Value of Agile Software Methods he explored the benefits that agile practices like pair programming or Test Driven Development can deliver.

Capers Jones has stated that "cost per defect penalizes quality" and "lines of code penalizes high-level languages" – these two metrics are harmful rather than helpful when it comes to setting goals for quality.

Is there a business case to be made for quality? Looking at the above investigations that is surely possible. Based on the investigations agile seems to provide significant benefits when it comes to quality (and not only for quality, also for speed and customer and team satisfaction).

If you want to build a business case for improving quality I recommend you read the book Economics of Software Quality by Capers Jones and Olivier Bonsignour. This book has software quality data that you can use to build a business case to improve the quality of your software and reduce technical debt, understand what influences quality, and decide upon processes and techniques that can help to improve the quality performance of your organization.

Another interesting book to read is The ROI from Software Quality by Khaled El Emam. It provides calculation models and data that you can use to decide where and how to invest in quality.

Software Quality is Free

In 1980 Philip Crosby wrote the book Quality is Free. In his book, he explained how investing time and energy in building the right products with good quality will save money and time. And how it will also make you cheaper and faster than your competitors.

Many agile teams know how important software quality is, but they need to convince their managers and other stakeholders to get time and space to work on quality, self-organize, and do their work in a good way.

More than 35 years have passed, and although the quality of software products has improved we are not there yet. We've moved from rigid waterfall processes to agile and lean approaches where people and collaboration are valued more than plans and processes. We're using feedback to learn and improve continuously. But we still see costly quality issues happening in IT.

> Having agile processes alone won't solve quality issues. But quality is still free. You need to have a quality mindset to delight your customers, and you will have to sell quality to your managers to help them to make the business successful.

Let's explore how you can sell that "quality is free" and build a business case for quality.

Understand your Customers

Quality is in the eyes of the users and customer. They value the products and services that you deliver, and they will pay what it is worth. You have to know why they want to have it. So quality starts with understanding your users and customers and their needs.

Next to understanding their needs you also need to be able to develop and deliver high-quality products and services. You need motivated people with good skills, processes and tools that help you to do the work, and a culture that supports getting the job done. This will help you to decide how you want to do the work that is needed to satisfy your user's and customer's needs.

Selling Quality to Managers

Selling quality isn't easy, but it's very important. If you want to improve the quality of your products and services then you have sell the importance of having a quality mindset and get your management to commit!

You need to have senior managers on board, make them aware of the importance of quality, so that they will support their agile teams when it comes to quality.

Managers have an important role when it comes to improving quality – managers should be driving quality to make it work.

Business Case for Quality

If you can show to your CxOs how the quality of your products serves the needs of his/her customers, then your CxOs will be sold!

Some ways to do this are:

- Highlighting cases where the quality of your product made a difference for one or more customers.
- Make visible where and why customers preferred your product above one from a competitor because of better quality.
- Know the price that you have paid for low quality, the time and money that you lost due to defects and technical debt.
- Have data showing how the higher quality of your product has saved time and money of your customers

- Gain an insight in the needs of your customers' customers (end-customers), know why they are buying the product and why quality matters for them.

These kinds of examples and cases will make clear that customers are willing to pay for quality, which makes a good business case to invest in quality and allow agile teams to find ways to develop and deliver high-quality products.

Agile Quality Practices

Since the agile values already support quality, and agile teams are highly collaborative, it is no surprise that agile teams deliver high-quality software. But how do they do it? Let's look at some practices for delivering quality software, that are applied by agile teams.

Collaboration with the potential users of the software is crucial to build a good understanding of what quality is. Scrum recognizes the role of the product owner, who defines the user's needs and focuses upon customer value. In the sprint planning product owners and agile development teams work closely together to define and prioritize the needs of the users, using user stories.

In the daily stand-ups, teams track their progress and raise impediments. My advice to team members is to bring up all quality issues. They can be discussed during the stand-up or if more time is needed in a separate session after the stand-up.

Pair programming is a practice performed by two developers sharing one keyboard and screen. One developer is typing, while the other one reads the code, signals potential problems and suggests improvements. During the session, they can switch roles.

With pair programming, the code is reviewed when it is typed, which gives quick feedback to the developer and prevents defects from entering the software at the earliest possible moment.

Another agile practice that increases product quality is Test Driven Development (TDD). If test cases are written before the code, then you know by executing the test that the code is working properly. The test cases are added to the regression test, so during the development, the agile team knows that the software remains correct.

Refactoring is a practice used to adapt existing code to meet current needs of the users.

> I suggest to only refactor when there is a good reason, for instance when you need to implement new functionality and the current code works against implementing it, or when there are many faults in a piece of code and rewriting is more effective that debugging or solving issues.

Refactoring can also be used to increase the performance of the product by optimizing the code to decrease execution time.

Team members need to develop their refactoring skills, so that they know how to update code efficiently and ensure the quality of the software product.

At the end of the iteration, a product review or demo is used to show the products and services that have been developed and get feedback. This feedback helps teams to increase their understanding of how the product should behave, and to spot problems which can be solved in a next iteration.

Agile teams continuously improve their way of working using agile retrospectives. By reflecting at the end of a sprint, the team looks for improvements and evaluates what they have learned. Agile has improvement embedded into the way of working, teams continuously learn and get better at what they are doing, increasing both their effectiveness and efficiency.

> My book Getting Value out of Agile Retrospectives provides different retrospective exercises that can be used to design retrospectives. It's a toolbox for agile coaches and Scrum masters which helps them to facilitate retrospectives that deliver benefits to the teams that they work with.

What If We Fail?

People are often afraid to make mistakes. They do things to prevent that something might go wrong and avoid doing things that might fail. And if it does go wrong then they don't talk about it.

The same happens when there's a quality problem with our software. People don't mention it because they are afraid they will get punished once their manager finds out that their software isn't working properly.

Is it really so bad if once in a while something goes wrong? If something could go wrong, let arrange for it to happen quickly as possible, because then you can learn from it sooner. Create a culture where failure is allowed so that we can all learn from it and find ways to make fewer mistakes!

What Are You Afraid Of?

Let's suppose that something goes wrong. What's the worst that could happen? Ok, there are situations and quality issues that you definitely want to avoid (for example, when human lives are at stake), but quite often it's not so bad if something goes wrong or if there's a bug in our software that we can solve easily and quickly. We still suffer the most from the fear of being ridiculed, but there's no need for that, so let's change that.

We also make it worse by blaming people for mistakes. Often that's a diversion, because let's be honest: who doesn't make mistakes? A culture in which you can make mistakes, in which you can honestly say that something went wrong, that you are unsure of something, is much more effective. In such cultures it is also easier to use the experience and strengths of employees to find solutions together.

Stop blaming each other, starting working together!

Fail Fast!

If things go wrong, you want to know about it quickly – to waste less time and money, and learn faster. It will fail anyway, so it's better if that happens now, and not in a few weeks or months.

> I recommend people to "test" risky things as soon as possible. For instance by working in an agile way to develop a first version of a product and ask your customers for feedback. Design a safe-to-fail experiment to try something new. Raise critical issues in a new partnership at the beginning to find out quickly if there are breakpoints which can endanger the collaboration.

If you are adopting a new way of working (for instance agile, Scrum, or Kanban), you can talk about it for weeks. But often it is more effective to just start doing it, and periodically evaluate (for example with agile retrospectives) how it goes. If things go well, then you will have a nice example of how it works, which you and others can learn from. If it fails, the damage is limited since you can take actions quickly.

Watch and Listen!

Often there are signals already at the beginning of a project that something is not going well. Ignoring them or postponing things doesn't help you, it's far better to fail fast and address the problems. You need to pay attention and you can observe a lot by just watching.

> Show that you appreciate it when people identify potential problems – do not shoot the messenger!

A short cycled improvement approach can be very effective to try something new. It helps people to listen better, to see the signs and mention them, and to become continuously better.

Learn From Failure!

So it's ok if failure happens. But it should not go wrong too often as you don't want similar problems happening over and over again (that is called insanity). Also when a defect has been resolved, you don't want the same problem to happen again in future releases.

Some suggestions to learn from failure are:

- Do a root cause analysis to deepen your understanding and avoid similar problems in the future.
- Use agile retrospectives to look back at what has happened, and agree upon preventive actions.
- Use self-organization and open spaces to involve employees in changing their way of working to do continuous sustainable improvement.
- Try a solution-focused approach, for instance with a strengths-based retrospective. This helps you to change by using your strengths.
- Use lean to identify waste and explore ways to tackle it using existing skills that people already have.

There are many good ways to learn from failure and mistakes, so I am surprised that there are still people who don't use them. Leverage your people and their strengths, empower your teams!

Reduce Mistakes and Improve Quality

Failure is essential in a learning organization. You need trial and error to deliver quicker and improve quality. You should not prevent failure but make it safe-to-fail. Learn from the mistakes that are made and prevent making similar mistakes in the future. But dare to try new things, don't be afraid to fail, it can only make you better!

Deliver High-Quality Software with Agile Teamwork

Effective agile teams are able to decide how to do their work and to continuously learn and improve their way of working. Teamwork enables them to deliver high-quality software that satisfies the needs of their customers. They can use techniques like swarming and pair working to solve complex problems quickly and reduce their technical debt.

Quality through Teamwork

How does agile teamwork help to deliver high-quality software? It has to do with multidisciplinary teams that are able to solve complex problems, driven by their motivation and empowerment.

> My opinion is that the whole team owns quality, which means that everyone on the team is responsible and accountable for their contribution towards delivering high-quality products. Give your teams the means to deliver high-quality software and allow them to self-organize and find out what works for them.

Most often quality issues are complex problems. They need to be viewed in multiple ways to solve them. Agile teams are multidisciplinary, they consist of professionals with different skills, knowledge, experiences, and backgrounds. Such teams have a diversity that helps to find innovative solutions and the know-how to collaborate for effective and lasting solutions.

Giving people freedom to decide how they will do their work will empower them. Self-organization gives freedom to teams.

In self-organized agile teams, motivation is often high since people feel that they are in control. Reaching the goal is what counts for teams and every team member will do the best (s)he can to get there.

Team Techniques for Quality Software

When there is a major issue, swarming can be used to address it effectively and quickly. The whole team focuses on a single issue and together they will do whatever it takes to solve it.

> Agile teams should have all the skills and experience that is needed to deal with problems effectively. They should know how to communicate and collaborate to get the job done.

Team members can work in pairs to increase the quality of the software while writing it. They can take turns on the keyboard, and switch to remain sharp and spot problems or opportunities to improve code and reduce technical debt. Pair working makes it possible for professionals to learn new skills or sharpen existing ones.

> If you're very deep into something, chances are that you start to overlook stuff – this is where pair working can help you. Also, two pairs of eyes can see more than one :-).

Managing Teams for Quality

Agile teams should be self-organized. They don't need managers to decide for them – telling them how to do their work isn't needed.

What managers can do to enable their teams to deliver high-quality software is:

- Make it crystal clear that quality matters to them.
- Reward teams that deliver high-quality software.
- Remove any impediments that teams bring up.
- Act as a servant leader to help their teams to be successful.

- Arrange for coaching and mentoring for teams.
- Allocate time for teams to learn and improve.

Learning to Deliver High-Quality Software

Software quality is free, teams that invest time and energy in building the right products with good quality will save money. Teamwork enables teams to deliver high-quality software.

Empower Teams to Increase Quality

When an organization is experiencing quality problems with their products, agile software development often isn't the first solution that comes up in people's minds. I see people trying to address them using classical waterfall based planning approaches, only to find out that it will make problems even worse.

Agile software development ingrains quality by applying visual management, using empowered teams and by inspecting and adapting to continuously improve the way of working. Therefore I recommend agile, not only to deliver working software faster but also with the right quality. This section shows how empowering the team helps to increase the quality of products.

Adding People Doesn't Work

In many organizations the solution applied when projects are experiencing major quality issues is to add more people to do testing, for fixing defects, or for whatever is needed. Unfortunately adding people never solves quality problems.

On a short term it always makes things worse: productivity goes down, more mistakes are made, and deliveries are delayed. In the long term it might work, but it's extremely unlikely. Chances are big that it disturbs the stability of teams.

Of course adding people to do testing or inspection will help to find more defects, and you need to find them before you can remove them. But you can't test quality in.

> Finding more defects when you already have a big list doesn't help to improve quality. It works better to resolve the defects that you have found already.

Adding people to solve defects helps to lower the number of resident defects, but there is a big risk that new defects are introduced if the new people do not know the software. Bad bug fixes are a nightmare, you don't want that on top of the quality problems that you already have.

Adding people either for testing or solving defects destabilizes a team. Team members will have to spend time to get to know each other and to help the new people to get up to speed. Brooks' law states that "adding people to a late project makes it later". Also the bigger the team becomes the more time it takes for team members to communicate and the overhead in the team will increase.

To conclude, adding people is never an effective solution to address quality issues.

Of course it is better to prevent big quality problems from happening, either by addressing them when issues are smaller and fewer, or by changing your way of working to assure that they do not happen. But if it's too late for that, when you are experiencing major quality problems right now, what can you do?

> To address urgent quality issues, my advice is to remove impediments that team members have. This allows developers and testers that are already on the team to solve more defects and solve them faster.

Work smarter, nor harder, is what works!

Diversity Matters

Most quality issues are complex problems. They need multiple views to solve them. Agile teams have the diversity that is needed to find solutions and known-how to collaboratively come to effective and lasting solutions.

Uniform teams with identical kinds of people would aim for steadiness and don't want things to change. Having diversity in agile teams makes it possible to discover and explore new ways of working – diversity enables continuous improvement.

When you are defining agile teams, make sure that they are multidisciplinary and diverse. This will enable teams to reflect and learn, and find better ways to do their work.

Empowerment Works!

What can managers do to enable their teams to solve the quality issues? Telling team members what to do is counter productive, in fact if they try it will create more problems instead of solving them.

To empower teams managers should work together with teams to remove any impediments that they have. By acting as a servant leader they can help their teams to be successful.

So next time when you are experiencing quality issues it is better to address them before they get out of control. Empower your team so that they can solve them effectively and quickly works better than adding people.

With agile self-organization, teams can increase their performance and capabilities to deliver high-quality products. No budget increase is needed – it is a matter of mindset, focus and giving attention and time to things that really matter: People!

Working at a Sustainable Pace

Agile promotes that teams work at a sustainable pace, delivering value to their customers. When teams are working under too much pressure, technical debt will increase and velocity of teams will go down. Agile retrospectives can help you to discover the causes of pressure, and to take actions to reach a sustainable pace with your teams.

A sustainable pace is a workload that teams can handle for a longer period, without compromising the quality of their products. It is based on a velocity that is doable for the teams and doesn't lead to stress or illness of the team members.

> When the workload of the teams becomes too high, chances are big that team members will make more mistakes with increased technical debt as an result. Team pressure drives code quality down and increases maintenance.

Due to the technical debt, the velocity of the teams will decrease so they will actually be delivering less value to their customers while putting in more hours. Clearly a waste of valuable time, money, and energy of your people.

Team Pressure

There's no work without occasional pressure, and having some pressure should be acceptable for teams. But if you have the feeling that your teams are always working under pressure, that the pressure is hampering your teams to deliver quality to your customers, then that is something that should be addressed.

> You can address team pressure in the agile retrospectives where team members can state how they feel that things are going, and use questions to discover what can be done to reduce the pressure.

A retrospective can also be used to find the root causes why team members feel that they are under constant pressure. You can do a five times why exercise to investigate the deeper causes.

Questions that you can ask to investigate team pressure are:

- Do teams get enough freedom to do the work in the way they think it should be done?
- Are team members allowed to make occasional mistakes and learn from them?
- Is it one or two person who are under pressure, or is it everybody in the team?
- How is the morale of your teams?
- Do team members feel happy when they come to work, and when they go home?

Using the retrospective you can find the causes of pressure, and take actions to address those in a next iteration.

Towards Sustainable Pace

If too much pressure due to a large workload is really hampering the team then the team should take action.

Possible actions that they can do are:

- Commit to a lower number of user stories in the sprint planning. Build in slack.
- Investigate which improvements teams can do to increase the team velocity.
- Establish stable teams which are capable of delivering quality products and maintaining high productivity.
- Prevent multitasking/task switching as much as possible.

- Monitor work in progress, use lean and Kanban to steer on flow instead of working more hours.
- Plan time for team members to relax and blow off steam after having had a busy period.
- Focus upon happiness in your teams, make sure that team members have fun while doing their work.

Collaborate with Stakeholders

It may be good to involve your stakeholders to find workable solutions to reduce the pressure and establish a sustainable pace that delivers value to them.

> Building trust is important: Stakeholders should trust the teams and assume that they will do the best they can, and the teams should earn this trust by continuously delivering valuable products.

In the longer run both the teams and the stakeholders benefit from a sustainable pace.

"If you want to deliver more, you should not work harder, but smarter" is a basic thing that didn't change when agile was invented.

The feedback and learning cycles from agile methods like Scrum can help you to improve. You need to invest time and energy, but when properly done it helps you to stop death marches, and to work at a sustainable pace.

Increase the Quality of Software with Visual Management

One of the principles behind agile and lean software development is transparency. Making things visible helps teams to decide what to develop and to collaborate effectively with their stakeholders and customers. It can also help to increase the quality of software.

Developing software with sufficient quality is something that many organizations are struggling with. Bad quality software manifests itself in many different ways, for instance by complaint from users, angry stakeholders, and unhappy developers.

> Insufficient quality leads to high maintenance costs and missed delivery dates. It impedes product innovation.

Quality is in the eye of the beholder, the users of the software and the customers buying it and the stakeholders who sponsor development. They will be the judge if the quality is good enough.

At the same time they are also the ones that can help agile teams to deliver better quality. All it takes is to make quality visible so that everyone involved can join forces to improve quality.

Visual Management in Agile

How can visual management help to increase the quality of the products when agile software development is used?

> My suggestion is to visualize quality: Show it to create a shared view and agreement between the teams and the stakeholders and customers. Visualization should radiate what needs to be done to ensure that the delivered products will have good quality.

Here are some suggestions for using visual management to increase quality:

- Using user stories the quality can be defined with acceptance criteria. They are a great way to explicitly state the quality that new functionality needs to have and to reach agreement on how the quality will be validated.
- Teams can use their Definition of Done (DoD) to define quality criteria that apply to all user stories. It helps to have the DoD visible at all times for everyone, e.g. by sticking it on the task board.
- The product demo (or sprint review as Scrum calls it) can be used to check if the quality of the delivered product meets the needs of the users. Where applicable teams can highlight quality aspects and ask for feedback from the attendees at the demo.

My experience is that visual management empowers teams to increase quality. Seeing things enables them to take good decisions on what to do and not to do to deliver high-quality software.

How to Visualize

There are many different ways to visualize things. Some of the ways to do it are:

- Make a drawing of a situation, problem, or solution (e.g. cause-effect diagram using root cause analysis or UML diagram for design).
- Present data on quality, for instance graphs with defect data or figures from static analysis tools.
- Brainstorm and write down ideas, then make them visible for everyone (e.g. with sticky notes or fishbone diagrams).

- Use a metaphor to bring out and organize information (e.g. sailboat retrospective, car brand).
- Gather data and use a graph to visualize it (e.g. burn down chart or team velocity).
- Use Lego Serious Play to model your ideas or way of working.
- Kanban boards are great for visualizing work. You can use physical boards with cards, of an online tool like Trello.

When you can get everyone involved in one physical location then you can easily visualize things using whiteboards or flip-overs. But don't worry, there are plenty of tools that you can use to visualize when working with distributed or dispersed teams. You can find some examples in the tools section of the retrospectives exercises toolbox.

One great book on visualization that I highly recommend is Visualization Examples by Jimmy Janlén. It's loaded with ideas on how to visualize things and it will inspire you to try new ways of visualization in your daily work.

User Stories for Quality Improvement

If quality is built in from start and teams and stakeholders pay attention to quality throughout product development, that's great. But sometimes quality is sacrificed and then you need to catch up and do an investment in quality.

User stories can be used to define and plan work that is needed to improve the quality of the existing product. Such a user story would have a quantified requirement.

Some examples of users stories to improve quality are:

- As a business owner of product xx, I want the yearly down-time to be less than 5 minutes, because that is the industry standard and expectation of our customers.
- As a user, I want the system to respond within less than 1 second in 95% of the cases, so that I can do my work effectively.
- The system should log all major outages (longer than 1 minute) and provide complete information so that the maintenance team can investigate them and take preventive actions.

When writing user stories for quality improvement always make sure that the business needs are clearly stated.

You don't want to do improvement for improvement's sake. There needs to be a solid reason to invest time and money. Make sure that your requirements drive quality.

Visualization Drives Quality

You can apply visual management to make potential quality issues visible early and to prioritize solving them.

The examples that I provided explain clearly why quality matters and how visualization can be used to establish, maintain, and increase the quality of software products.

Reduce Software Maintenance

Maintaining software programs costs a lot of time and money, which organizations would like to invest in developing new software that brings value to their customers. But how can you reduce software maintenance, and lower technical debt? By throwing your bad software code away!

The suggestion to throw bad code away that I describe below is inspired by a blog by Jerry Weinberg on Disposable Programs. Thanks again Jerry for the gift that you have that brings out good things in people.

Throw Bad Software Away!

Here's my suggestion for dealing with bad code:

> To say "no" to bad quality software you have to throw old smelling software code away. Just go into your configuration management system, isolate the software modules that are costing you lots of time and money to maintain, and delete that code.

Ok, maybe you cannot simply delete and throw away bad code. Your software products will not work anymore, your users will complain (even more than they do about the current buggy software product), and you run the risk of getting out business quickly.

But let's think about it: Why do we keep software code that is unmaintainable, keeps us awake at night, that hinders us in developing software our users really need?

Reasons that I often hear are:

- We are afraid to throw code away as we might need later.
- We've spent so much time and money, we don't want to lose our investment.

- We can always improve it later, let's keep it for now.
- We don't have the time and money to throw it away and develop new code.
- We can't come to a decision to throw it away.

It's easier to non-decide (and to keep bad code) than to decide to throw it away. It takes guts to do it. But I don't think there are any good reasons to keep bad code smelling – you have to deal with it.

My advice is to dispose bad code as soon as possible to not waste time and money.

Refactoring

If you are not ready yet to throw it away, then refactoring may be a suitable solution for you to reduce your maintenance. Use it to rewrite parts of your software to make the code more maintainable, to be able to implement new functionality, or both.

Agile software development has embraced refactoring as a technique to reduce the technical debt. Refactoring is one of the most valuable techniques that I know to improve the quality of code.

Sampling for Code Quality

Sampling the quality of your code with reviews is a way to measure the quality of your code. By reviewing just a part of a software, and measuring the defects that are found (both number of remarks and severity), you can extrapolate the data to determine what the quality of the code is.

For instance, if you find 15 defects in 250 lines of code, and the total module size is about 1500 lines, then you can expect to have around 90 defects in it. Multiply that with cost of finding and solving a defect, and you know how much the maintenance costs will be. Are you willing to pay that much in the future?

It is cheaper to review and rewrite code – it prevents costly defects being reported by the users of your products.

Make the Decision!

Most people hate making decisions, and are afraid to make the wrong decisions. This is in my opinion one of the root causes why we have so much horrible software.

When you keep on having problems with a piece of software, throw it away. If it really feels as a loss, re-create it, then you will have a better version.

If it doesn't feel that you lost something (and your users also don't miss anything), then there is no problem so you did the right thing to throw it away. Leave it like that, and invest your time in more valuable things.

I've had several occasions in the past where I lost a program, a piece of documentation, a blog text or a presentation by accident. I didn't feel good when it happened, and of course I tried to get it back. Finally, I had to give up and decide to rewrite it. The second version has always been better, and took only a small amount of time to create it. Why? Because the thinking done to create the first version was most of the work. Creativity was my biggest investment, typing it didn't take much time.

When I lose my code or text I still have my investment, so my loss is very limited. And when I re-create it, I often get new insights which made it even better.

> Since I became aware of this I, dare to stop searching and make a decision to recreate. Also when I don't feel happy with something, I just delete it. I'd rather invest my time in making something which is valuable, and use my strengths to deliver to my customers. It makes me feel better to deliver valuable results quickly. Which is also something that my customers appreciate :-).

Measure Defects

Measuring defects can provide you with valuable information about the quality of your product, but measuring alone doesn't improve quality. You need to dive deeper to have a good understanding and then act upon that.

Measuring to Take Action

Sometimes people measure defects because they are easy to measure. But not everything that can be counted, counts. As with any measurement, there must be a reason why you measure it.

> Measuring can make sense if you want to steer and improve quality of your product – managing quality in an economical way.

Measuring defects should only be done if it serves a purpose, like:

- Analyzing those defects (for instance using root cause analysis) that provide information where to improve your process and then take action to prevent similar defects in the future.
- Knowing what the quality of the product to be delivered will be and take early action if that quality will be insufficient.
- Improving collaboration between designers and testers by having them discuss defects and agree upon the actions that they will take together to improve quality.
- Helping your stakeholders to balance between quality and functionality. Help them to decide when to invest in testing, in reviews, and in defect prevention.
- Manage your technical debt to reduce software maintenance and ensure that you are able to deliver new functionality and value to your customers.

Measure Quality with Agile Teams

You can measure and steer quality in agile teams. When you are using agile, I've found it to be effective to discuss quality risks already in the sprint planning. At that time, the product owner and the team can discuss the process that they will use, which practices they think are most effective, and what the expected quality of the product will be.

Estimates and metrics of defects can help you to discuss expectations, and get early warning signals.

I urge people to change their estimate when they have reasons for it. Don't use estimates as commitment – use them to build understanding and to facilitate good discussions between those involved in quality!

You can't manage what you can't measure. But you must make sure that you only measure what is relevant. Otherwise it's like looking for your keys under the lamppost, not because you lost them over there but because the light is better which makes it easier to search.

Make sure you only measure what you need. Use your measurements: do proper analysis, discuss the results with those involved, decide, and take action!

Improve Software Quality with Retrospectives

An agile retrospective is a practice for teams to reflect, learn, and to continuously become better in what they do. Although retrospectives are mostly used to explore the current way of working, they can also be used to investigate quality issues or to agree upon actions that can improve the quality of the software that is delivered.

Explore Problems with a Root Cause Analysis

The five times why retrospective exercise uses root cause analysis to identify the deeper causes of quality problems. The basic technique is to build a shared view of the cause-effect tree, by repeatedly asking "why". Each cause that is identified by asking why is listed on the tree, and then questioned to find out why it happened, until you find the lowest or root causes.

When you're at the fourth or deeper level in one of the branches of the tree you often get to a situation where nobody knows the answer (this is as it is), or there is no need to go deeper: Now you have found a root cause!

Note that there often are multiple causes why something happened. You want to have a complete view of all causes before deciding upon actions.

Once you have identified all root causes then you ask the team for actions that would prevent similar causes to happen in the future.

> Be careful to not have too many actions, agree upon the Vital Few Actions that are most urgent and effective.

Five times why is one of the retrospective actions that is described in my first book Getting Value out of Agile Retrospectives

Building an Awesome Product Futurespective

A futurespective is a retrospective where you start from the goal to find ways how to get there.

Teams place themselves in the future by imagining that their goal has been reached.

Next they will discuss their imaginary past and explore how they have gotten to their goals, by exploring the things that have helped them to get there and the things which made it hard to reach their goal.

Now teams go back to the present, and the results from exploring their imaginary past are used to agree how to work together to reach the goal.

Here's how you can do a futurespective to explore ways to build an awesome product:

1. Imagine that it's half a year from now and you just heard back from the users of your product that they are extremely happy with it. It's the best quality software they ever had, it makes their work easier and saves them time. It's easy to use, flawless, fast, flexible: Everything they expected, and more.
2. Take some time to celebrate this to get into the right mood. Be excited, do a team hug or high fives, give compliments to each other, grab a drink – whatever makes you happy.
3. Imagine what you have done to deliver high-quality software. Which practices did you use and how did you do them? How did you work together as a team, with your stakeholders, customers, and users? What have you tried that worked out well?
4. Also, imagine the problems that you had along the way and how you dealt with them.
5. Now go back to the present, and use the things that have come up to define your way of working.

Reflect with the Agile Self-Assessment Game

The Agile Self-Assessment Game can be used by teams and organizations to self assess their agility. With this game, teams can discover how agile they are and what they can do to increase their agility to deliver more value to their customers and stakeholders.

> The basic game and the expansion packs contain many cards that can be used to discuss quality practices that your team is using or might use.

Playing the game helps you to see how well you are doing and to find ways to improve the quality of the software that you deliver.

Solve Quality Issues with a Stop the Line Exercise

The concept of "Stop the Line" comes originally from the Toyota Production System. It is a lean technique where anyone is allowed (actually urged) to stop the assembly line when a problem is discovered.

Start the exercise by creating an "andon". It can be a rope tied to a large bell or a button connected to something that will generate a heavy noise when pushed. You can also ask the team to shout out and yell when a team member steps forward to report a problem.

Ask team members to reflect on the iteration and to recall a moment when they saw a problem. When a team member has one, (s)he should stand up, go to the andon, and let the team know.

The team member will briefly explain the problem, where the retrospective facilitator will summarize it on a flipchart or whiteboard to make it visible to everyone.

Once there is a collection of problems, the team decides which one they want to eliminate (for instance using dot voting). Next the problem is analyzed to find the root causes and define actions for the next iteration that will prevent similar problems.

My advice is to either time-box the retrospective or up-front agree upon the maximum number of actions that you want to have. This will ensure that the retrospective will lead to valuable improvements and that time isn't wasted.

Those who know lean will be questioning why the line is stopped in the retrospective, which isn't what Taiichi Ohno intended. And yes, you are right:

Agile teams should stop the line anytime when any team member sees a major problem. The real benefit that this exercise brings is that it teaches you to see problems early, dare to stop and signal the team, and take action.

My advice is to put Andon in your team rooms so that at anytime team members can walk over and use it to stop teams when there's an issue.

Effective Agile Retrospectives

If you want to increase the value of your agile retrospectives, here are some things that you can do:

- Read the book Getting Value out of Agile Retrospectives and use the Retrospective Exercises Toolbox – they both provide valuable exercises for your retrospectives.
- Attend a workshop on Valuable Agile Retrospectives in Teams or Increasing your Agility with Retrospectives.
- Read my blog posts on retrospectives.
- If you're stuck, then reach out and ask your agile retrospective question.

All these things can help you to spice up your agile retrospectives.

Root Cause Analysis in Software Development

Root cause analysis (RCA) can be used in software development to build a shared understanding of a problem by identifying all the causal relationships. Knowing the evidenced-based causal relationships helps to identify effective improvement actions to prevent similar problems in the future.

You can also do root cause analysis in agile to stop problems that have been bugging your teams for too long.

Root cause analysis can give a significant boost to reaching business targets on increased quality, reduced delivery time and lower costs. Understanding the causes and taking action drives software product quality.

Success Factors for Root Cause Analysis

There are many different ways to find the root causes of problems. You can do an extensive problem analysis involving one or more professionals and present the results to those involved to discuss and refine them. For smaller problems you can do a five times why exercise where you explore the problem to find all relevant root causes to take action.

> Analyzing defects that have been found in test or reported by customers helps to control the quality of your products. Agile teams can do root cause analysis in the retrospective or have a separate session where they deep dive into a problem by asking why.

Regardless of the techniques or exercises that are used, it is important to do root cause analysis effectively – you want to get business value out of it.

Just Enough Sessions

When you start with root cause analysis it can be tempting to investigate every problem. You may think that the more sessions you do the better.

But that will result in too many actions, which your organization probably can't deal with. You are wasting time coming up with actions that will not be done and are overloading your organization. That's insanity, stop it!

Instead of making the selection for actions after doing a root cause analysis, you want to do just enough sessions to come up with a minimal number of valuable actions that your organization can cope with – to ensure that you only do high beneficial actions.

> For any problem that is to be investigated with a root cause analysis, the loss must be significant in terms of business value.

> There must be a significant chance that similar problems will occur that lead to losses in the future if no preventive actions are taken. If not, then don't do a root cause analysis.

Knowledgeable Facilitator

To do root cause analysis effectively the facilitator has to focus on the process and the culture in the meeting.

> I've seen good results when experienced quality or process managers facilitate root cause analysis sessions. They have the skills to lead the analysis, know about product development, understand how their teams work, which processes they use and how they use them, and they speak their language.

The interaction between the facilitator and the attendees in the root cause analysis is crucial. They need to have the same technical, process, and organizational background in order to come up with the real root causes. And of course soft skills matter to get good actions out of a root cause analysis.

Having root cause analysis sessions attended by people who have worked in projects and maintenance for a long time can be very effective. Typically such professionals recognize potential causes which might be overlooked by people who have less experience.

Communicate the Actions

Of course it isn't over after the root cause analysis session. On the contrary, this is where the real work starts, by doing the preventive actions that came out of the session.

Communication plays a very important role to change organizations and enable continuous improvement.

Preventive actions must be taken up and completed. Communicating the actions and the expected business results supports implementing the actions. People will know which actions are done and (very important) why. They will be more willing to support the actions if they are aware of the problems that they prevent, and the benefits that they will bring.

Root causes and actions should be communicated broadly, preferably to all people working in projects or departments where the root cause analysis was done. This helps professionals to learn from problems that others have had and to be better prepared when similar problems occur to them.

My advice is to communicate how the preventive actions from root cause analysis have contributed towards reaching the targets of the organization, preferably in quantified terms. Communicating the results gives buy in for future actions and helps to see the benefit of doing them.

In the end, the business results should make it worthwhile to do root cause analysis, and keep on doing it!

Agile Root Cause Analysis

Agile provides optimal conditions to do root cause analysis. You can steer product quality in agile by analyzing defects that are found during an iteration. Improvements in the way of working can be introduced in a next iteration during the sprint planning.

Agile retrospectives can help to further optimize the usage of root cause analysis. They provide the means for teams continuously improve themselves and increase the value that they deliver. Organizations that want to improve their processes with a combination of agile and CMMI can apply root cause analysis using the CMMI.

I've seen the value of root cause analysis in all kinds of organizations, high and low maturity. There are always defects and problems that you can learn from and use that to improve your way of working. The investment to start with root cause analysis is low, and you start getting benefits quickly.

Develop Your Software Quality Skills

I regularly provide public workshops and training, and in-house classes tailored to specific situation and needs of organizations.

Effective Root Cause Analysis

In the *Workshop Effective Root Cause Analysis* you will learn practical and effective techniques to analyze problems. You will practice these techniques using major defects or problems from your own organization.

What will you get out of this workshop:

- Understanding the why and how of root cause analysis.
- Experience how to do root cause analysis.
- Learn how to define actions to prevent problems.

Valuable Agile Retrospectives

In the Workshop Valuable Agile Retrospectives you will practice different kinds of retrospective and learn how to adopt and apply retrospectives in your own organization.

What will you get out of this workshop:

- Understand the why, what and how of agile retrospectives.
- Practice different retrospective exercises.
- Learn how to create a safe environment to run retrospectives.
- Practice skills for facilitating retrospectives.

Getting More out of Agile and Lean

In the Workshop Getting more out of Agile and Lean you will experience agile practices for teams and stakeholders with advice on how to deploy them, and tips and tricks to increase your agility.

What will you get out of this workshop:

- Practice sprint planning, stand-ups, demos and retrospectives.
- Improving collaboration in teams and between teams and stakeholders.
- Tips and tricks to improve your agile way of working.
- Advice on selecting and applying agile practices effectively.

Agile Self-assessment Game

The Agile Self-Assessment Game is used by teams and organizations to self assess their agility. Playing enables teams to reflect on their team interworking and take the next steps in their agile journey.

With this game, teams discover how agile they are and what they can do to deliver more value with high-quality software.

The card of the Agile Self-assessment Game are based on the manifesto for agile software development and generally accepted agile principles and practices. This makes the game useful for all agile team, whether using Scrum, Kanban, XP, Lean, DevOps, SAFe, LeSS or any other agile framework.

You can download the game and expansion packs in my webshop.

Attend a Workshop

See my upcoming workshops for attending a public workshop.

Contact me if you want to have an in-house workshop tailored to the needs of your organization.

More information, see Services Ben Linders Consulting.

About the Author

Ben Linders: Trainer / Coach / Adviser / Author / Speaker

Ben Linders is an Independent Consultant in Agile, Lean, Quality and Continuous Improvement, based in The Netherlands.

Author of Getting Value out of Agile Retrospectives, Waardevolle Agile Retrospectives, What Drives Quality, and Continuous Improvement. Creator of the Agile Self-assessment Game.

As an adviser, coach and trainer I help organizations with deploying effective software development and management practices. I focuses on continuous improvement, collaboration and communication, and professional development, to deliver business value to customers.

I'm an active member of networks on Agile, Lean, and Quality, and a well known speaker and author.

I share my experiences in a bilingual blog (Dutch and English), as an editor for Culture and Methods at InfoQ, and as an expert in communities like Computable, Quora, DZone, and TechTarget.

Follow me on twitter: @BenLinders.

Bibliography

My Blog and Books

Ben Linders - Sharing my Experience - www.benlinders.com

Getting Value out of Agile Retrospectives

What Drives Quality

Register your book at benlinders.com/what-drives-quality

Books (Ordered on Title)

Adrenaline Junkies and Template Zombies: Understanding Patterns of Project Behavior by Tom DeMarco et al.

Apollo Root Cause Analysis by Dean L. Gano.

Commitment: Novel about Managing Project Risk by Olav Maassen, Chris Matts, and Chris Geary.

Competitive Engineering by Tom Gilb.

Continuous Delivery by Jez Humble and David Farley.

Economics of Software Quality by Capers Jones and Olivier Bonsignour.

Effective Debugging: 66 Specific Ways to Debug Software and Systems by Diomidis Spinellis.

Fifty quick ideas to improve your user stories by Gojko Adzic.

Getting Value out of Agile Retrospectives by Luis Gonçalves and Ben Linders.

iTeam: Putting the 'I' Back into Team by William E. Perry.

Management 3.0 by Jurgen Appelo.

Managing for Happiness by Jurgen Appelo.

More Agile Testing by Janet Gregory and Lisa Crispin.

Product Mastery by Geoff Watts.

RealityCharting by Dean L. Gano.

Reinventing organizations by Frederic Laloux.

Scrum: The Art of Doing Twice the Work in Half the Time by Jeff Sutherland.

The Business Value of Agile Software Methods by Dr. David F. Rico et al.

The Clean Coder by Robert C. Martin.

The Digital Quality Handbook by Eran Kinsbruner.

The Lean Startup by Eric Ries.

The Mythical Man-Month: Essays on Software Engineering by Fred Brooks.

The ROI from Software Quality by Khaled El Emam.

The Software Craftsman by Sandro Mancuso.

Turn the Ship Around! by David Marquet.

User Stories Applied by Mike Cohn.

Visualization Examples by Jimmy Janlén.

Links

Manifesto for Agile Software Development

retrospectives.eu

Retrospectives Exercises Toolbox

Agile Self-assessment Game

www.ingramcontent.com/pod-product-compliance
Lightning Source LLC
Chambersburg PA
CBHW031947190326
41519CB00007B/705